BRITAIN IN OLD PHO

AROUND SOMERSET

From the Montague Cooper Collection

Nick Chipchase

First published 2008

The History Press
The Mill • Brimscombe Port • Stroud • Gloucestershire • GL5 2QG

Reprinted 2011, 2013

Copyright © Nick Chipchase, 2011

Title page photograph: The artistry of H.M. Cooper. His two daughters shown as a composite of four.

British Library Cataloguing in Publication Data
A catalogue record for this book is available from the British Library.

ISBN 978-07509-4677-3

Typeset in 10.5/13.5 Photina.
Typesetting and origination by The History Press.
Printed and bound in England.

Maid with dog. One of the thousands of untitled studio portraits by Henry Montague Cooper.

Contents

	Introduction	5
1	Taunton	9
2	Villages Around Taunton	25
3	The Bridgwater Area & the Quantocks	57
4	Burnham, Highbridge & District	75
5	Minehead & North Somerset	95
6	Wellington, Wiveliscombe, Milverton & District	121
7	Wells, Glastonbury, Wedmore, Chard & Ilminster	141
	Acknowledgements	160

Montague Cooper's studios.

Henry Montague Cooper (1864–1945), photographer.

INTRODUCTION

Henry Montague Cooper was born in Cheltenham in 1864. The 1881 Census lists him as Harry M. Cooper, aged seventeen, assistant to his father William who was a furniture dealer and valuer. Young Harry left home shortly after this and moved to Taunton. The Cooper family were comfortably off. Their home was at Ashley Villa, Cheltenham, where William employed three servants. One of these, a 'nurse domestic', aged fifteen, was employed to care for Henry's brothers Thomas, aged three, and newborn Ashley. Another fifteen-year-old maid helped William's wife Mary run the household.

Henry Montague Cooper and his brother left home as teenagers. The brother became successful in the furniture trade and after a short while, in the same business, young Henry met and married Jane Morley whose father, William, was an established Taunton photographer. Jane (known as Jenny) was a Catholic and they married in 1888. Around that time William Morley decided to retire and the young couple acquired the photographic business.

William Morley was born in Oxfordshire in about 1823 and had built up a flourishing business in Taunton, specialising in studio portraits, stereo views of the town and commissions to photograph local properties. The Coopers carried on in a similar vein, trading under the title H.M. Cooper late Morley. They lived at the studio

H.M. Cooper business letterhead.

Taunton studio interior, c. 1914.

at 27 East Street (later no. 29). Henry dropped his forename within a few years to become Montague Cooper. He considered himself to be a 'photographer made, not born'. Nevertheless, he was an astute businessman with a passionate interest in new technology and methods. Jenny was an accomplished photographic artist who had learned the trade from her father. Together they made a successful team.

The Coopers had no children of their own but lived with two 'nieces', supposedly the daughters of Henry's late brother. In fact they were the illegitimate daughters of H.M. Cooper by Harriet Fanny Ellis, who worked in the Taunton studio. Mary Agnes Cooper was born in about 1897 and her sister Gladys slightly later. Both births were registered at Exeter and the father's name given as 'Henry Montague'. Neither Gladys nor Mary knew their true identify until they were adults. Mary's children were not aware of the situation until after her death, aged ninety-one in 1988. Mary helped her 'uncle' in the studios. She was at the Burnham studio at the start of the First World War and took photographs of soldiers before they were posted to the front. Sadly, some were killed before the negatives had been filed away.

It is quite remarkable that Jenny should bring up the girls under the cover of their being nieces. It is obvious they were never going to be told their true parentage, as the facts were later discovered by chance. Mary had learned this when she needed a passport to travel to Australia after her husband's death. However, this was at a time when illegitimacy was considered more shameful than it is today.

Business prospered for Henry and Jenny. By 1901 they were able to employ a servant and embark on foreign holidays. It was on such a trip to the continent that Henry became aware of the picture postcard trade. He could not wait to get home to examine the prospects of such work. This he discussed with other members of the trade, including the Holes of Williton. The families appear to have been friends, as Bert Hole of Watchet was staying with the Coopers at the time of the 1901 Census.

Although Henry Montague Cooper's business motto was 'be first in the field', his were not the first postcards sold in Taunton. The earliest recorded postmark for the town is dated 18 October 1899. This on a multiview postcard published by Valentine. Mr Cooper's earliest known postcard is of the Royal Train passing Taunton on 25 August 1902 (see page 14). In 1902 the Post Office allowed the sender of a postcard to write a message on the address side. This left the other side entirely for the image. From this time until about 1910 postcards were produced in many millions. Not only were they useful for messages, they were also avidly exchanged and collected by people all over the land. They were also an important means of conveying pictorial news in the days when few newspapers carried photographs. The astute and rapidly mobile local photographer had a great advantage in this field.

Montague Cooper was one of the first businessmen in Taunton to acquire a motor car. His earliest appears to have been a 3½ h.p. Benz. Licensing records from 1904 reveal a series of cars bought by Mr Cooper. In 1903 he owned a De Dion two-seater (Y94) but soon upgraded to a M.M.C 9 h.p. (Y308); a 12 h.p. Belgica (Y388) soon followed. All three appear in postcard views, parked up, while the photographer sets up his equipment (usually accompanied by a posse of children).

From recorded postmarks it appears that Mr Cooper embarked on a massive accumulation of topographical views in 1904.

The motor car carried him to all parts of Somerset west of the Mendip Hills. The early postcards were much in the style of Francis Frith and were printed in monochrome in Germany. This was not uncommon at the time, as it was cheaper. Taken as a whole over the thirty years of postcard production, Mr Cooper's work falls

Taunton studio interior, *c.* 1914.

into four distinct categories. The earliest and most prolific work was almost entirely topographical and covered the period 1902–7. These postcards included villages, towns, major country houses and over 200 Somerset churches. Copyright photographs were also supplied to a number of local businesses to produce their own postcards. Around 1908 Mr Cooper's studios started producing local real photographic cards. This social history era lasted until the First World War and included the 1911 Coronation celebrations, political events, sports, shops and a multitude of other local subjects.

The emergence of the postcard trade also coincided with the expansion of Mr Cooper's business. He had acquired a new studio at The Esplanade, Burnham, by 1897, followed by Victoria Street, Burnham; High Street, Wellington (both by 1906); then Wembdon Road, Bridgwater, and High Street, Chard, soon after. A branch was also opened at Lynton, North Devon, in about 1900. Mr Cooper made sure his postcards were on display in every railway station within 60 miles of Taunton.

The First World War saw a new era in postcard production and studio work. The postcards featured views of army manoeuvres, weapons, hospitals and encampments. The Taunton studio was kept busy with Australian soldiers requiring photographs to send back home. Many asked for snow scenes which the photographic artists faked by flicking solution on to the negatives. Nearly every soldier being sent away had the customary photograph taken of him in uniform. Similar work was carried out at Burnham but the studio had to close when the German manager was interned. After the war there was a brief revival of the social interest postcard, but the number and quality of work never matched that of the early days. A royal visit to Taunton was covered in 1922, as was the dedication of various war memorials. Also there was some interest in Empire Day and pageants, but the golden era of postcards had gone. The latest known Cooper cards are those for the Bridgwater and Taunton pageants of 1927 and 1928.

Although heavily committed to the production of commercial photographs, Mr Cooper never relinquished his interest in photography as an art form. He was elected President of the Professional Photographers' Association in 1914 and featured in their journal of June 1914, together with prize-winning photographs (a copy was kept by Gladys). In portraiture, Mr Cooper favoured the light 'sketch portrait'. A cabinet head, vignetted on a whole plate sheet of paper, with a delicate background put in by airbrush. He enjoyed making composite studies, as shown on the title page, where his two 'nieces' are shown as a group of four. His studios also catered for the amateur photographer, offering Kodak camera films and accessories together with a printing and developing service.

In about 1929 the Coopers decided to retire. Montague was now in his mid-sixties and they moved to a bungalow on the Blackdowns (the Croft at Clayhidon) and later to 7 Central Avenue, Paignton. For many years the glass negatives had been carefully wrapped and filed away in the cellar at Taunton. Fortunately, they survived a disastrous fire there in about 1921. Mr Cooper sold them all to Miss Phillips, a worker at the studio, for half a crown. Her father tried to find a long-term home for them, but nobody was interested. Eventually he destroyed the lot. Gladys took most of the full plate negatives of the Somerset churches, supposedly all those in the Diocese of Bath and Wells, to Brentford. They were stored in Harriet's attic, but fearing a bomb strike during the war would bring them crashing through the ceiling, they had them destroyed.

Nobody has had the foresight to preserve the work of Henry Montague Cooper. All we have left are some of the earlier studio photographs and those of the millions of postcards he produced that have withstood the ravages of time.

1

Taunton

Election results at Shire Hall, 1910. This Declaration of the Poll took place on Tuesday 25 January 1910 in front of a large crowd of people. The incumbent MP for West Somerset, Sir Alexander Acland-Hood (*see* page 126), had beaten his Liberal opponent Mr Walker-King by 1,066 votes. The following day Sir Alec addressed his supporters from the portico of the Castle Hotel (*see Taunton in Old Photographs*). The Shire Hall, a Victorian Gothic building designed by William Moffatt, was built between 1855 and 1858 to house the Assize and Quarter Sessions.

London Hotel. Taunton.
Proprietor, E. H. Claridge.
Head-Quarters of the Automobile Club.
'Phone. 0134.

The London Hotel, c. 1904. The two postcards on this page illustrate Mr Cooper's skill at altering photographs. The occasion is a rally organised by the De Dion Bouton Motor Company in July 1904. The man on the tricycle is Tom Crump, surveyor to the Rural District Council. Ernest H. Claridge took over the hotel in 1901 when he was thirty-one years old. He was assisted by his wife Susan and they employed a barmaid, two hotel book keepers, a kitchen maid, a housemaid, a chambermaid, a cook, an under chambermaid, a pantry maid, a page boy, a boot cleaner and billiard maker.

LONDON HOTEL, TAUNTON.
Proprietor, W. F. Whittingham.
Large Assembly Hall for Banquets
Balls and Theatricals.
Telephone, 134.

Walter Whittingham, a local wine and spirit merchant, bought the hotel in 1913 and continued to use the same postcard (now altered) for advertising. Whittingham had acquired Scarlett & Sons wine and spirit merchants business in nearby Cheapside at about the same time. After his death in 1919, his widow sold the hotel to Trust Houses Ltd who renamed it the County Hotel.

The London Hotel, c. 1914. This multiview postcard shows interior views of the hotel. It stands on the oldest recorded public house site in Taunton (The Three Cups, 1528). In about 1912 Taunton's second cinema, the Empire, opened in the assembly hall.

Marshalsea's Garage, Fore Street, c. 1912. Left to right are a Darracq, Fiat and Hallford. Mr Van Trump is the figure on the right. As well as charabancs, Hallfords also built lorries and buses. Darracq were originally a French company, until taken over by Owen Clegg in about 1913. A merger with Sunbeam Talbot came in 1920. Fiat originally stood for Fabbrica Italiana Automobili Torino (F.I.A.T). Marshalsea Brothers originally started their business at Ilminster and had acquired premises at 55 East Street, Taunton, before January 1911 (*see* page 157).

The new post office, North Street, c. 1911. The post office had formerly been located in Church Square. This new building was constructed at a cost of £7,000 by Pollard and Son of Bridgwater on the site of the Spread Eagle Inn. It opened for business on 19 March 1911. The clock was added two months later, funded by the Town Council and by public subscription. The postmaster at Taunton supervised eighty sub-post offices, fifty-one postmen and forty-eight sorting clerks and telephonists. In 1910 there were five weekday deliveries from 7 a.m. to 7.30 p.m., and one on Sunday.

In 1908 an interesting case came before the court. The Postmaster General had agreed to pay £3,000 for the Spread Eagle Inn. A dispute arose over terms and conditions in which the defendants, William Hancock and Company, Brewers, were awarded judgement against the Postmaster General.

Lathe and turning works, *c.* 1910. Mr Cooper has left us no clues for this business but it is believed to have been in Taunton. Postcards like this were not produced by the national photographers and one wonders at the commercial value for such a venture. Perhaps it was a special commission for the company involved.

The opening of Park Fountain, 31 October 1907. The ceremony was conducted by the Mayoress, Mrs Augusta Sibley, and the corporation. It had arrived rather late as it was intended as a memorial to Queen Victoria. It was a busy day for the mayoral party, as from here they moved on to open the new Station Road extension and North Town School. In recent years the fountain was renovated with the help of old postcards as the Town Council did not retain the original drawings.

The Royal Train at Taunton, 25 August 1902. This is the earliest known postcard published by Cooper. It is an undivided back early type of postcard. Who was actually on the train we don't know. The king and queen were at the Portsmouth Naval Review on 23 August. They then proceeded by Royal Yacht to Scotland calling at Weymouth on the way.

The First Taunton Tram Run, 21 August 1901. It seems there was a rush to complete the tramway, as the council received numerous letters of complaints up to its opening regarding conditions on the roads. On the day, technical difficulties meant that the first run did not take place until 5.00 p.m. Two cars were decorated by W. and A. Chapman Ltd, and carried 2,000 people during the evening's run. After inauguration, further letters of complaint followed regarding the Sunday tram service. The Town Council hoped that a compromise could be made so that the trams did not run during Divine service. There were further complaints in November when two cows were knocked over.

East Street Drapery fire, 1908. This was the worst fire in Taunton for twenty years. It started in the kitchen at the rear of the drapery at about 2.30 p.m. on Sunday 12 April. The fire quickly spread to the shop area and Mr Love, the owner, his wife and family, together with seven shop assistants, had to flee the building.

Edward Love was born in Taunton in about 1857. In 1888 he bought 23 East Street and converted it into a drapery and millinery shop. The premises were extended by the addition of 21 East Street. The rooms on two floors above the shop were used by Mr Love, his family and the lady assistants.

Taunton Fire Brigade attended the scene and the tram service was suspended as a large crowd of onlookers assembled. Much of the building and nearly all the stock was destroyed. The fire was still smouldering at 5.30 p.m. Both premises and stock were insured and Mr Love was back in business with a spring sale just one year later.

The Duke of York's visit, 1922. Mr Cooper produced at least twelve cards of this visit to Taunton on 20 June 1922. The Duke of York, the future King George VI, visited the town as he was Colonel-in-Chief of the Somerset Light Infantry. He presented the DCM to RSM Grange at the SLI Depot and had a brief tour of the town in a 19 bhp Crossley car supplied by Taunton Motor Company. At the Municipal Buildings he was met by the mayor, Cllr F.S. Dodson and his corporation. The 5th Battalion of the SLI provided a guard of honour as the loyal address was read. The duke also visited the Castle Hotel where Mr Cooper took a number of photographs. After lunch at the barracks, the duke returned to the station to continue his journey to the West Country.

The duke's next visit to Taunton would be as King George VI on 2 December 1937. This was an unofficial visit en route to the Duchy of Cornwall. On a wet day the king was received by the Marquis of Bath in the station car park.

George V Coronation dinner, June 1911. Celebrations started at 7.30 a.m. with peals of bells at St James's, St Mary's and Wilton churches. The dinner for over-sixties was held at the Market Hall. This was decorated with garlands of artificial flowers and evergreens. Mr J. Hawkings of the Railway Hotel provided the luncheon, which included roast and boiled beef, boiled hams, plum pudding, cheese, butter and salad with hot potatoes. Local breweries donated beer and mineral waters. The dinner was accompanied with music from the 5th Somerset Territorial Band playing in the street outside. The day ended with fireworks and the lighting of beacon bonfires across the county.

Market House and Taunton centre, c. 1904. This is a less common viewpoint of the town centre which has been photographed by many postcard publishers. The Market House was built in 1770 but its arcades on the side were removed in 1930. The Kinglake Memorial (centre) was erected in 1867 and demolished in 1934. At this time a market was held on the Parade on Wednesdays and Saturdays but it moved to a new site off Priory Bridge Road in 1929. Taunton has now lost its market town status as a new market site has been built near Bridgwater.

Holt Tractor, Station Approach, c. 1917. Mr Cooper certainly had an interest in things mechanical and produced a number of postcards showing the Holt. This one is the 15-ton Holt introduced in 1917. The caterpillar track seen here was invented by a British company in 1905. Holt Tractors of California bought the patent and developed tracked vehicles, mostly for agricultural use.

Holt Tractor and gun in East Street, c. 1917. After evaluation, the British Army imported a total of 232 Holts to haul the heavy guns. This gun appears to be an 8-in Mark 1 Howitzer. It used shortened and bored-out naval 6-in guns mounted on traction engine wheels. Five marks of this design were made, but the improvised nature of the gun led to failures such as premature explosion and unreliability in action. Early versions of the 8-in shells were also unreliable. The fuses failed so often that the battlefield was littered with unexploded shells.

Holt and Howitzer at Taunton station, *c.* 1917. The 15-ton Holt agricultural tractor was petrol-driven. Essentially, it was a half-tracked vehicle with a separate steering front wheel. Despite its 20-ft length, the Holt had a turning circle of only 10ft. They were slow and noisy with unshrouded engines, almost straight-through exhausts and steel-on-steel track assemblies.

Holt at Taunton station, *c.* 1917. The writer of this card states that 'the caterpillar is leaving for Southampton'. The army's first order of 200 machines had been delivered between November 1917 and April 1920. A 20-ton Holt tractor eventually replaced the 15-ton version and was used by artillery units up until the early 1930s. The Holts were used by the various heavy and siege batteries of the Royal Garrison Artillery. These companies employed 60-pounder guns, 6-inch and 8-inch Howitzers and the static 9.2-inch Howitzer.

Gun carriages at Rowbarton, *c.* 1917. The writer states 'this is not an eight-inch Howitzer, may be a new type of six-inch.' If this is so, this would be the 6-inch, 26cwt Howitzer introduced in 1915. This replaced the two earlier versions and went on to become one of the British forces' most important weapons in the First World War. The wooden-spoked wheels could be fitted with 'girdles' to stop them sinking in the mud.

Holt tractor and WD lorries at Rowbarton, *c.* 1917. The British Army were impressed by the idea of a tracked vehicle in 1909, but did not develop the idea. In 1914 Colonel Swinton considered the possibility of modifying an armoured vehicle to carry caterpillar tracks and set about convincing the British Government of the merit of his idea. In 1915 William Tritton invented a new kind of flanged track that would not droop when suspended over a trench. The tank was thus born, although early use on the battlefield was far from successful.

Gun at Rowbarton, *c.* 1917. This appears to be a 9.2-inch Mark 1 heavy siege Howitzer. This one belonged to the 79th Brigade, the Royal Garrison Artillery. The Mark 1 Howitzer was first produced in 1914 and 450 were built between 1914 and 1918. It weighed 15 tons, took 36 hours to dismantle and was moved on three specifically built carriages. The Howitzer could fire a 288lb shell a distance of 5.7 miles.

Maypole Dairy at 33a Fore Street, 1916. 'Standing by himself is our Charlie'. This is Charlie Boon, later employed as a motor driver, who committed suicide by jumping into the canal. The inquest into Charlie's death was recorded in the *Somerset County Gazette* on 19 March 1927. The tall lady in the centre is Ada Knill, the butter patter. The people in the photograph are, left to right: Victor Moore, Mabel Baker, manager, Eva Templeman, Ada Knill (née Bond) and Charlie Boon.

A carnival float in St Augustine Street, *c.* 1908. The proprietor of the St Augustine Street Collar Works, Mr Henry J. Van Trump, is second from the right. The works were known as the Tone Vale Manufacturing Company and were built in 1898. A number of postcards were produced by Mr Cooper for successive years' carnival entries. They won first prize in 1907.

The Italian singers' carnival entry, *c.* 1908. Mr and Mrs Van Trump are on the extreme left. H.J. Van Trump was born in North Petherton in about 1846. His wife was Elizabeth (née Stone). His 1901 Census address was 59 East Street, where he lived with his wife and four children. They employed a cook servant. Mr Van Trump was Mayor of Taunton from 1916 to 1920, during which time he lost his son Harry, who was killed in action. Harry had previously survived an aeroplane crash with Henri Salmet when they ditched in the sea at Minehead in 1914.

The funeral of W.H. Askwith, 1911. William Henry Askwith was born in Leeds in about 1844. He was Archdeacon of Taunton and Vicar of St Mary's Church for twenty-three years. The funeral service was held at St Mary's Church, the Revd Askwith's coffin having been made by his precentor Mr T. Doble. The extensive funeral procession was led by the choir, churchwardens and clergy pallbearers. Then followed the chief mourners, the mayor and corporation, borough magistrates, market trustees, governors, teachers and pupils of Huish and Bishop Fox's Schools.

W.H. Askwith lived at St Mary's vicarage with his wife and sister, together with their two nephews. They employed a cook, parlour maid and housemaid. Shortly after Askwith's death, a memorial school was built at South Street (the author being a former pupil).

The proclamation of George V at Taunton, 1910. A large crowd assembled in the centre of the town. The chief constable called for silence for the high sheriff who presented the proclamation to the mayor to read out. This was followed by a fanfare. The Union Jack was raised and the band played the national anthem. The High Sheriff then called for three cheers from the crowd.

The Priestman Canal Dredger, c. 1905. Montague Cooper produced this advertising postcard for Priestman Brothers of Hull, engineers and mechanical grab manufacturers. The dredger is shown at work on the canal near Firepool. This dredger was purpose-built for such work. An alternative was a standard dredger mounted on a pontoon or barge. Priestman excavators are almost legendary in the business. The company became part of the Acrow Group in 1970. A copy of this postcard currently holds the record for a Montague Cooper photograph at £150.

2

Villages Around Taunton

Coronation bonfire and Mr Eland Clatworthy, 1911. The photograph was taken at Trull or Cutsey nearby. The Clatworthys lived at Fairlawn House. In 1902 it was written that 'the expression of joy by means of bonfires has been natural to all ages'. This came to a peak between 1887 and 1911. 2,500 bonfires were lit for Queen Victoria's Diamond Jubilee in 1897. A central committee was formed in 1902 to establish a National Bonfire Union to organise the 3,000 bonfires for the king's coronation. All the bonfires were to be lit simultaneously. Similar arrangements were made in 1911 for the coronation of King George V. An illustrated book was published that year called *The book of the Coronation bonfires*.

The hunt at Stoke St Mary, *c.* 1905. The village is mentioned in a Saxon charter dated 854 AD. It is situated some 2 miles south-east of Taunton. The church was built in the thirteenth century and remains largely unchanged, having one of the few remaining thirteenth-century towers in the county. The Half Moon Inn is still a popular public house. In 1901 the innkeeper was George Jemmet who lived here with his wife and eight children.

Henlade House, *c.* 1904. Henlade is a hamlet in the parish of Ruishton, just outside Taunton. The house stands in its own extensive grounds and was built in 1805 by an Italian architect. In 1901 it was occupied by widow M.C. Clarke Preston, her daughter and six servants. By the time the photograph was taken, the occupier was H.E.M. Anderson. The property is now run as the Mount Somerset Country Hotel.

Hestercombe House, *c.* 1906. The house is a Grade II listed country house just north of Taunton. It was originally built in the sixteenth century for the Warre family. The building was enlarged and altered in the eighteenth century and further extensive work was carried out in about 1875 for Edward Portman, 1st Viscount Portman, who had acquired it in 1873. The house remained in the Portman family until 1944. The gardens were landscaped for E.E.B. Portman by Gertrude Jekyll and Edwin Lutyens between 1904 and 1906.

Funeral of E.W.B. Portman, 1911. When the 1st Viscount died in 1888, the 2nd Viscount made over Hestercombe to his son, Edward W.B. Portman. E.W.B. Portman's coffin was carried through the estate on a wagon drawn by a team of horses. The 2nd Viscount Portman lived until the age of ninety in 1919, but his son Edward had died in 1911. His widow continued in residence at Hestercombe until her death in 1951, though the freehold of the estate had passed to Crown Estate in 1944.

Barton Grange, *c.* 1905. The building lies on the Corfe and Pitminster parish boundary. This was the site of the Prior of Taunton's summer residence, which was purchased at the Dissolution by Humphrey Colles. What remains is only a fraction of the original building, as the house was reduced in size at the beginning of the nineteenth century and further reduced in 1931. As small boys we used to sneak into the cellars while the house was uninhabited. Local rumour stated that there was a tunnel from here to Poundisford Park.

Blagdon village, *c.* 1905. In the centre is the Mission Room, built in 1878, and just behind this is the gable over the entrance to the Lamb and Flag Inn. Behind the cottages on the right is the former White Lion, then owned by Hanbury and Cotchin. The landlord was William Warren, who was also the local wheelwright.

Fitzhead church and village, c. 1905. Fitzhead is a parish and village 3 miles east of Wiveliscombe. The church is dedicated to St James. The village population is currently around 250 and it still retains its popular pub. The main residence is Fitzhead Court, once the principal residence of Lord Ashburton, who was responsible for the building of Wiveliscombe Town Hall in the late nineteenth century.

Burrowbridge, c. 1905. Here the River Parrett is overlooked by Burrow Mump and the ruins of St Michael's church. The river bridge was built in 1825 from blue lias blocks with a granite arch and parapet. Burrowbridge was the last toll bridge in Somerset; it was 'freed' in 1946. In 1921, tolls raised £252 and by 1925 it had reached £513. This from the 3d given to the gatekeeper (the original act of 1821 stated 'for every horse, mule or ass drawing, three pence').

Church Row, Bishops Hull, *c.* 1906. This row of cottages is opposite the church. The village is almost a suburb of Taunton now, but the centre retains some of its old-world charm. The cottages could not be located on the Census by name, but Percy Merson lived in no. 1 during the First World War. He formed a group of lady bellringers for St Peter's Church.

Taunton Vale Harriers, *c.* 1905. At this time Mr John White, JP, of Leacroft, was master. The Harriers originated from a pack formed by Mr James Scarlett, formerly landlord of the Nags Head in North Street, Taunton. The pack pursued hares during the season which ended in March. Their country included Fivehead, Isle Abbots, Blue Ball and Bishops Lydeard. For the latter, the Letherbridge Arms served as a meeting place. Mr White retired as master after four years' service in 1908 and was succeeded by Mr G.W. Hodgkinson.

Trull village, c. 1905. Trull is a parish and village 2 miles south of Taunton. The church is dedicated to All Saints and in the late nineteenth century the tower was rendered in plaster. The village still retains its primary school and the author attended the school. The population in 1901 was 960, but this has now increased to over 2,000 due, in part, to the village's proximity to Taunton.

Trull post office, c. 1904. Albert Bull was postmaster at this time. In about 1908 the hedge was removed and a wooden study, formerly used by the vicar, was sited here and used as a post office. The building continued in use until about 1960. Letters arrived at 6.45 a.m. for Mr Bull to sort and a second batch arrived at 3.00 p.m. The post office is now situated at the top of Church Road. Just beyond the post office is the village shop, which is still in existence today.

Churchinford, *c.* 1905. The village lies in the parish of Churchstanton and sits 10 miles equidistant from Taunton, Honiton and Chard. Churchstanton parish was transferred from Devon to Somerset in 1895. The ancient names of Churchinford were Cheltona and Chestonford. The village sits where six roads meet and is designated an Area of Outstanding Natural Beauty.

The York Inn, Churchinford, *c.* 1905. The building dates, in some parts, to the sixteenth century and still retains an open fireplace and oak beams. Walter Doble held the licence at the time of the photograph. He was a local man and ran the inn with his wife, Jane, and a teenage servant.

Pitminster village and church, c. 1905. Pitminster is a village and large parish 4 miles south of Taunton. It includes Blagdon, Lowton, Staplehay and Eastbrook. The parish church is dedicated to St Mary and St Andrew. The parish population in 1901 was 1,262 in an acreage of 5,274. There were schools at Pitminster and Blagdon and post offices at Lowton, Pitminster and Blagdon.

Pitminster post office and school, c. 1905. Miss Joan Upham was postmistress in 1910. Although born in Pitminster in about 1852, the 1901 Census places her in Paddington, employed as a lady's maid. The post office (the thatched building) was damaged by a fire in 1955 and a new house was built for Mr and Mrs Lee, the occupants. The school (centre) was built in the parish orchard in 1840 and catered for 101 children when it opened. With numbers declining, the school closed in 1921, reopening briefly during the Second World War for evacuee children from Plaistow.

The ford at Combe Florey, *c.* 1905. This view of the ford is from the Minehead road. It has long since been replaced by a bridge. The horse is definitely out of scale and must be Mr Cooper's little bit of fun. Like other small Quantock villages, Combe Florey has literary connections. The writer and famous wit, the Revd Sidney Smith, lived here and the Waugh family bought Combe Florey House in 1956. Both Evelyn Waugh and his son, Auberon Waugh, are buried in the village. There are twenty-four listed buildings here, including the Elizabethan gatehouse next to the church.

Combe Florey village, *c.* 1906. In the distance is the school – now a private house. The school was built in about 1848 and subsequently enlarged to accommodate seventy children. At this time it was run by Thomas Lilley and his wife. The village population was 260 in 1902. At that time, it had no post office and no public house within the village, though there were two blacksmiths and a small village shop.

The Vicarage, North Curry, c. 1904. The building dates to the early eighteenth century. Daniel Pring lived here with his two children. The Revd Mr Pring was ably supported by three servants in the household – two housemaids and a cook. After the First World War, the Revd Mr Pring initiated a scheme to build the village war memorial.

North Curry, c. 1905. This view was taken from the old brewery. Behind the tree is Queen's House, which housed Dare's bakery in later years. The cottage on the left at the end of the green is Flagstones, at 23 Queen Square – a Grade II listed building. (For the opposite view see page 36).

North Curry, c. 1905. This is the reverse view of the photograph on the previous page. On the extreme left is London House, where Thomas Giblett had a shop which appears in directories from 1889 to 1923). He produced his own postcards of North Curry. The gas lamp was replaced by a war memorial in 1920. The old brewery is the building to the right, which is a Grade II listed building originating from the late seventeenth century. James Temlett was the occupier at this time.

Lydeard St Lawrence, c. 1906. This view up the hill shows Court Farm on the left. The house on the right is St Bees which has now been obscured by the later Pond House. The village grocery shop is in the centre of the photograph. Lydeard St Lawrence is a small village and parish 5 miles north-east of Wiveliscombe on the Taunton to Minehead road.

The stocks in Creech churchyard, *c.* 1905. Stocks were used as a punishment or humiliation as early as Anglo-Saxon times. The second Statute of Labourers (1350) ordered the punishment for unruly artisans and decreed that they should be set up in every village. Stocks were used until the early part of the nineteenth century, though some later records show their use as a punishment right into the 1860s.

Langaller, *c.* 1905. Langaller is a hamlet in the parish of Creech St Michael. Since the motorway was built, this little section of road has been left as a cul-de-sac. The photograph has been taken close to Langaller Manor, which was at this time home to retired farmer John Richards and his wife Gertrude. The Richards family also owned Langaller Farm. James Pendry, florist and seedsman, also ran a business in the hamlet in the early twentieth century.

The Tone Bridge, Creech, c. 1906. No doubt there has been a bridge on this section of the Tone for many centuries. The old wooden bridge, probably on stone piers, was replaced by this stone bridge in about 1800. In 1848 Edward Murch of Bridgwater removed the parapets and replaced them with iron girders and railings. Murch was also responsible for the building of the bridge between Hurst and Martock and Bridgwater Gas Works.

Creech: a bird's-eye view, c. 1906. This is a view towards the village from the embankment of the old Chard Canal. The road to Ham is situated to the right of the pedestrians. In the background are the New Inn and the church. The north-east chapel is the oldest part of the church, having been built by the Cluniac Monks of Montacute in the thirteenth century.

Creech, North End, *c.* 1905. These two photographs illustrate quite clearly Mr Cooper's method of work. He has arrived by car and attracted a group of inquisitive children. These have happily posed while both photos were taken near the same position. This view shows North End with Laurel Villa on the left. Just out of view to the right is Northend Mill, owned at this time by Joseph Loader, the water coming from the Preen, which runs through Northend.

Creech Heathfield, *c.* 1905. The children have moved closer to the camera. On the left is Northend Farm. This was owned by Frank Richards, originally from Ruishton. It seems likely that he had not been here long as four of his five children were born outside of Creech. This actually is the road to Creech Heathfield, which is a hamlet in the parish of Creech St Michael. Here the Crown Inn was run by Oliver Leach, a member of a well-known local family of innkeepers, carpenters and shoemakers.

The Durston rail crash, 1909. This accident occurred at about 1.00 p.m. on a Saturday in March 1909. The goods train involved had left Bristol bound for Plymouth. It was one of the biggest engines on the system, hauling eighty trucks all laden with goods. As the engine approached Cogload Junction at Durston the leading twelve wagons became detached from the engine and those that followed. The trucks flew in all directions; some were smashed to pieces while others ran down the embankment, spilling the goods they contained. Damage was done to both Up and Down tracks. A breakdown gang was telegraphed and dispatched from Taunton.

Shortly after the accident, the West Country mail train was halted nearby and delayed for four hours. Rather than receive late mail the Taunton postmaster dispatched two 'powerful' cars to the scene. These were provided by Messrs Beech. They carried thirty-seven mailbags

back to Taunton for sorting and delivery. The Down line was blocked for most of the Saturday. About 100 men were engaged in the clearance and a crane was used to lift the wrecked trucks. The accident drew a large number of visitors to the scene, including our photographer Mr Cooper.

The photographs show mixed stock. Included are a 4–4–0 locomotive similar to a City class, a 388 double-framed Armstrong goods and a 388 Class no. 794 with Swindon boiler. The cranes are a 10-ton hand crane on a six-wheeled chassis and a 6-ton crane not in use. The trucks include 12032, built in 1888; 73903 built in 1900; and 76452 built in 1907. The larger stock includes a permanent way train, brake van, an 'iron mink' steel van and a six-wheel engineer's coach in 1908 chocolate livery.

Hatch Green, *c.* 1905. Hatch Green lies just to the south-west of Hatch Beauchamp. Two weirs were built here when the mill stream was constructed. The stream fed the Higher Mill in Hatch Beauchamp village. There were two bridges at Hatch Green: one called Bottle Bridge, the other Pot Bridge. Also in the photograph is Hatch Green Farm.

Hatch station, *c.* 1905. The station is a Grade II listed building and now a small industrial site. The station is situated just south of the 152-yard Hatch tunnel on the Taunton to Chard branch. It was built between 1864 and 1866. The main building is of brick with ashlar dressing and a Welsh slate roof. The station had a single platform on the Down side and a goods loop on the Up side. The signal-box was built on the Up side of the goods loop. The 13¼-mile branch line opened in 1866. In 1956 the goods loop and signal-box closed, and as a result of the Beeching Report, passenger traffic ceased on the whole branch in 1962.

Hatch Court, c. 1905. The house is described as one of the most outstanding examples of Palladian architecture in the whole county. It was built of Bath stone in 1750 by Thomas Prowse of Axbridge. The gardens at Hatch Court have been lovingly restored in recent years, including the spectacular walled vegetable garden which adjoins the churchyard. This, along with the deer park, is a reminder of how this part of Somerset appeared almost three centuries ago.

Hatch Baptist Chapel, c. 1905. Teaching of the Baptist faith at Hatch dates back to the mid-seventeenth century. The chapel was built in 1783. A later register for the chapel includes burials for 1837 to 1929, a list of graves, and also marriages for 1838 to 1905. A history of the chapel notes the deaths of John Yard, aged ninety-two, a member of the chapel for fifty-seven years, and of his son James, one of the deacons, who died in 1829.

Hatch Beauchamp, c. 1905. On the left is Henry Fry's Hatch Inn. The gateway on the right leads to Beauchamp Lodge, home of Mrs Raben. Henry Fry ran the inn with his wife, Harriet. He employed two servants. The village is 6 miles from both Taunton and Ilminster. The village is the burial place of Colonel John Rouse Merriot Chard, VC, hero of Rorke's Drift (1879).

The White Hart, Corfe, c. 1904. Thomas Bond, then twenty-five, ran the inn in 1901. He was a local man who shared the accommodation with his wife, Bessie, and her unmarried sister, Lily Bond. Starkey, Knight and Ford owned the premises between the wars. The road on the right leads to Pitminster.

Corfe looking south, c. 1904. Corfe is a village 4 miles south of Taunton. In 1901 it had its own post office, church, chapel and school. The population was 383. The chapel, visible on the left of this photograph, was built in 1897 and is now a private house.

Corfe vicarage and school, c. 1904. In this view, looking north, the vicarage is on the right. Montague Cooper's MMC car stands in the road. Peter Brancker was the vicar and he lived here with his wife, Florence, employing three servants. In 1898 the vicar had electric lighting installed in the church for a cost of just over £53. The school accommodated ninety children from Corfe and Orchard Portman. The school had electricity installed in 1904. The building is now a private house and a war memorial stands where the elm tree is.

Halse village, c. 1906. Mr Cooper produced four charming photographs of the village. It seems quite clear what happened. He arrived by car and parked it outside Halse House, possibly starting work at the school and going around the village trailing all the children behind him. They were only too happy to pose in the photographs.

Halse is a parish and village 7 miles south-west of Taunton. The church here is dedicated to St James. The population in 1902 was 356, and at that time the village had a post office, shoemaker, blacksmith, baker, grocer and draper and one inn. The post office was sold in 1939 together with the Manor House, three farms, Halse Manor Mill, nineteen cottages and the village carpenter's shop.

The New Inn, Halse, c. 1905. On the right are steps and the doorway to Culver Cottages, which no longer exist. Alfred Sawyer was the innkeeper at the New Inn. Aged sixty-five in 1901, he originally came from Sussex. His wife Elizabeth was local, having been born at Thurlbear. Like many publicans at this time, Alfred could afford to employ a young single woman as a servant.

The school, Halse, c. 1905. The building dates from 1856 and thirty-five children attended here in 1905. Indeed, most of them seem to have followed Mr Cooper around during his visit. The school was given to the education authority in 1939, when the estate was sold by the young Lord of the Manor, Hugh Graham Evelyn Dunsterville.

Halse Manor, *c.* 1906. The building is Grade II listed and dates back to the seventeenth century. It was enlarged in the mid-eighteenth century and remodelled in the late nineteenth century and again some seventy years later. In the 1980s it served as a hospital but has since been converted by Messrs Wrencon into fifteen individual houses and apartments with no. 12 set within the former coach house.

Mrs Eland Clatworthy and carriage, *c.* 1909. This particular carriage is a phaeton, of which there were numerous types.

The Square, Bishops Lydeard, c. 1904. The name above the shop doorway states 'Comer Sadler'. The Lethbridge Arms, formerly the Gore Inn, takes its name from the Lethbridge family who lived at Sandhill Park from 1767 to 1913. In 1901 Joseph Heydin and his wife, Mary, ran the pub. They employed locally-born Florence Gange as a general servant. In the pub car park is a well-preserved Fives wall.

Frog Street, Bishops Lydeard, c. 1905. The row of cottages on the left were gutted by fire in April 1906 and subsequently demolished. Montague Cooper's 12hp Belgica Y388 is parked in the road. The car was a twin-cylinder model built by a cycle company established in Brussels in 1885. The company exhibited a six-cylinder 58hp model at the 1908 Agricultural Hall Show in London.

A bird's-eye view of Bishops Lydeard, *c.* 1905. Bishops Lydeard is a village and parish 5 miles north-west of Taunton. The population here was 1,105 in 1905, but unlike many villages in the area it has risen considerably to nearly 4,000 today. These two views were taken from the church tower and give views of both the village and Somerset landscape of 100 years ago. The A358 to Minehead now bypasses the village. Bishops Lydeard also lies near the West Somerset Railway and the village station is an important staging post on the line. Regular trains run from here via Watchet to the terminus at Minehead.

A view from Mount Street, Bishops Lydeard, c. 1905. The girls are standing at the entrance to Brookside. Beyond here is Church Street with the 107ft tower of St Mary's Church in the background. The church dates mainly to the fourteenth and fifteenth centuries and was extended between 1860 and 1862 by Jeboult of Taunton. The churchyard contains a cross dating to the fourteenth century, as well as the town's market cross which was moved here in the nineteenth century.

Kingston Green, c. 1905. Miss E.B. Cheetham of Tetton House planted the oak tree on 13 December 1897 to commemorate Queen Victoria's Diamond Jubilee. It still stands to this day.

Kingston St Mary village, *c.* 1904. The thatched cottages in the background were demolished in about 1920. The gabled building housed Amphlett's Kingston Stores in 1909 (*see* page 123, *Taunton Remembered*). The car Y308 is Montague Cooper's 9hp MMC, which he acquired in 1904. The Motor Manufacturing Company was established by H.J. Lawson, initially in Coventry. Production ceased in about 1908 after the company had moved to Clapham. A 12hp Belgica replaced the MMC after a short while.

Kingston St Mary – a bird's-eye view, *c.* 1905. Kingston St Mary is a parish and village 3 miles north of Taunton. It lies under the southern extremity of the Quantock Hills. The parish once belonged to the kings of the West Saxons, hence its name – 'The Kings Settlement'. Only in the 1950s was the name of the village church, St Mary's, added to the village name. The splendid west tower of the church was built in 1490.

Kingston St Mary, c. 1905. Also known as Hills or Hill Farm, the listed building is now part of a select redevelopment project. Montague Cooper photographed most of the main Kingston houses at this time. The owners in 1901 were the Bucknell family, of which William Bucknell was the head. He was born at Ashbrittle in 1831. His wife, Anna, nearly ten years his senior, came from West Monkton. William Hurman owned the farm in the 1950s.

Tetton House, Kingston St Mary, c. 1905. Tetton House and its terrace to the front garden is a listed building. This view shows the building, which dates from about 1790, before it was partly rebuilt and enlarged between 1924 and 1926. The work was undertaken by H.S. Goodhart-Rendell for H.M. Herbert. Some interior features are of note, including a dramatic ashlar-fronted stair hall and two fine, imported eighteenth-century marble fireplaces. F.H. Cheetham JP lived here in 1902.

The Club, Norton Fitzwarren, *c.* 1904. The village club was erected in 1896 at a cost of £1,000 by W.G. Marshall Esq. William George Marshall was Lord of the Manor at that time. The bowling alley was added in 1897. The recreation ground adjoining the club was opened in 1920 as a memorial to the twenty-two men of the parish who fell in the First World War. The building now serves as a village hall.

A bird's-eye view of Norton, *c.* 1904. Where possible, Mr Cooper would climb to the top of the village church tower for his 'bird's-eye views'. This scene is very different now. Taunton Cider's premises were built right across the centre of the view, but all of this was demolished in 2007 for residential development. The gardens in the foreground have also been filled by modern houses. Certainly the many elm trees in the distance no longer remain.

Norton Fitzwarren coronation pageant, 1911. The pageant was organised by Mr and Mrs Stenlake and seven historical episodes were included. The first episode featured a battle between Romans and Britons at Theodunum (the old name for the camp at Norton). Other episodes included Alfred burning the cakes, Blake defending Taunton in 1644 and Dick Whittington and his cat. The final tableau was Britannia accompanied by patriotic solos. Sports and dancing followed together with a dinner for 330 people.

Monty's Court, c. 1904. The house was built for Sir John Slade in 1836. The stable block bears the date 1838. 'Monty's' is not a name, but a reference to a house in a glade or glen. Wyndham Slade JP was its owner in 1901. At this time the house was only occupied by servants, Wyndham Slade being at his London house at 88 Chester Street on Census night. The present owner is a descendant of the Slades – Major A.C.W. Mitford-Slade. His father, Lieutenant-Colonel Cecil Townley Mitford, adopted the Slade name by deed poll in 1941.

St Augustine's Church, West Monkton, *c.* 1905. The building dates mostly from the fifteenth century and the tower is similar in style to those at Norton Fitzwarren and Cannington. The pillars and buttresses are built of Ham stone and much of the walls consist of Devonian slate or Monkton ragstone, the latter probably having been quarried locally. Like the church at Trull, the tower may have been plastered at some time in the past. The clock is an old timepiece recorded as far back as 1747 when three of the bells were recast. As with other Somerset churches, the churchyard contains stocks and an ancient yew tree. Montague Cooper photographed most, if not all, of the churches in the Diocese of Bath and Wells in about 1904. It must have taken an enormous amount of travelling to accomplish this.

3

The Bridgwater Area & the Quantocks

The Quay, Bridgwater, c. 1906. The town's name most likely comes from the Old Norse 'Bryggia', meaning quay or jetty. This photograph shows the west quay. It is thought that there were discharging facilities at Bridgwater on both sides of the river as far back as 1200. The construction of the west quay dates to before 1730. The cart in this photograph bears the name Bell and Son, House Furnishers.

River and bridge, *c.* 1906. A bridge at this site also dates to around 1200. A new bridge was constructed in 1400. This stone bridge was itself replaced in 1798 by an iron bridge cast at Coalbrookdale in Shropshire. Increased traffic and the bridge's steep approaches meant that it eventually became unfit for purpose and the current bridge was subsequently made by George Moss of Liverpool. It opened in 1883.

The war memorial, Bridgwater, *c.* 1924. The memorial was sculpted by John Angel and unveiled on 25 September 1924 in King Square. The central figure is 'Civilisation', seated like a queen on her throne. Under her feet are the figures of 'Strife', 'Bloodshed', 'Corruption' and 'Despair'. On her lap she supports the Book of Law and in her right hand is an orb in the shape of the world. Four figures on this orb represent the four corners of the world. Two guardian angels guard the book on 'Civilisation's' lap. The angel's wings form a canopy at the back of the design sheltering small groups of figures, 'Labour', 'Education', and in the centre, 'The Home' – the main supports of 'Civilisation'.

The commission came rather later than the others in the country, probably owing to the length of time taken to secure the public subscription and the long decision over the proper site. King Square was being restored at the time but a huge crowd gathered for the moving ceremony of unveiling and dedication by the Earl of Cavan. The commission was worth over £2,000 to the sculptor, Angel.

St Mary's and Cornhill, Bridgwater, c. 1905. The market building and the landmark dome were built in 1823 by Mr Thomas Hutchings of Bridgwater. This is the real heart of the market town. The statue of Admiral Blake was unveiled on the Cornhill in 1900 by Lord Brassey. Public subscriptions raised over £1,200 for the casting of the bronze statue. The 175ft spire of St Mary's has dominated the Bridgwater skyline since 1367.

The free library, c. 1906. The library was opened in September 1906. It cost £3,500 to construct, the money coming from the world-famous Carnegie Foundation (the same source which funded the Taunton library in 1904). The building was constructed on the site of Binford House from the plans of local architect E. Godfrey Page, son of E.T. Page, local publisher and photographer.

Departure of the Army Service Corps, Bridgwater, c. 1915. Here we see the Army Service Corps (ASC) passing the Home and Colonial Stores. Another name given to the ASC was 'Alley Sloper's Cavalry', as they were the unsung heroes of the British Army in the First World War. The ASC operated the army's transport, ferrying huge amounts of food, equipment and ammunition to a vast number of men on many fronts. Other companies of the ASC were responsible for the supply of horses and manual labour.

Waiting for orders, Bridgwater, c. 1915. Behind the men is Croker's Tobacconist. Montague Cooper was clearly interested in such comings and goings and produced other postcards of the 'Terriers' at the station, the West Somerset Yeomanry and 'recruits for Lord Kitchener'.

Bridgwater Pageant, 1927. The pageant was held in June and depicted scenes of famous people and notable events in the history of Bridgwater and the surrounding district. It took place in the grounds of Sydenham Manor and involved 1,000 performers. Donations and receipts for the pageant totalled over £1,865 and the profit of about £440 was donated to charity. A pageant procession through the town preceded the main event at Sydenham Manor.

Over Stowey, schools and vicarage, *c.* 1906. Over Stowey village is a small affair clustered around the church. The parish, however, is quite large and includes the hamlets of Plainsfield, Aley, Adscombe, Friam and Bincombe. The Stanley family of Quantock Lodge paid for the church restoration in Victorian times when several windows designed by the famous artist Edward Burne-Jones were installed. William Holland was vicar here from 1779 until 1819 and some of his diaries were published as a book entitled *Paupers and Pig Killers* – a picturesque account of the life of the village. His view of Somerset folk was that they were 'of large size and strong, but in my opinion very slow, lazy and discontented.'

St Mary's Church and clock tower, Nether Stowey, c. 1906. Nether Stowey is a busy village just off the A39 between Minehead and Bridgwater. Its bypass was constructed in 1968 and the older part of the village is a conservation area. The village is famous for its links with the Romantic Poets Samuel Taylor Coleridge and William Wordsworth. The clock tower in this photograph was built for Queen Victoria's Jubilee in 1897.

Castle Street, Nether Stowey, c. 1906. Henry Routley's shop can be seen in this view. The street takes its name from the eleventh-century motte-and-bailey castle at the top of the village. The castle was destroyed in the fifteenth century, possibly as a penalty for the local lord's involvement in the Perkin Warbeck rebellion against the Crown. Lord of the manor Lord Audley was executed in London after being paraded around the city dressed in a paper coat. The state of the road suggests that it was the road sweeper's day off.

Coleridge's house, Nether Stowey, c. 1905. The original building was a small cottage containing a parlour, kitchen and service room on the ground floor, with three bedchambers above. The cottage was refurbished in 1800 and extended later in the nineteenth century. After Coleridge left in about 1800, the building eventually became Moore's Coleridge Cottage Inn. It was acquired for the nation in 1908 and handed over to the National Trust.

Fire damage at Halswell House. c. 1925. Halswell Park was developed between 1745 and 1785 as a setting for Halswell House, which was built in about 1690. The house was originally purchased by the Tynte family. The property was featured in *Country Life* magazine on 21 November 1908 and the fire occurred sometime in the 1920s. Much of the estate, including the house, was sold off in 1950, and part of the property was converted to flats. In 1985 it was again sold and the Halswell Park Trust was established with the aim of restoring the house and grounds. Now owned by Dunster Investments, it has become an exclusive wedding venue.

Stogursey village, c. 1905. Mr Cooper has attracted his usual crowd of children in Stogursey's wide main street. The village lies 3 miles from the A39 and the village of Nether Stowey. It is only a mile away from the sea. The village was given to William de Falaise by William the Conqueror and is recorded as Stoche in the Domesday Book. The village became Stoke Curci or Courcy and is now Stogursey. At the end of the street the church of St Andrew can be seen; it was built in the early twelfth century by English, rather than Norman, builders.

Stogursey National School, c. 1905. The school was designed by John Norton for Sir Peregrine Acland, who gave the school to the community in 1860 as thanks for the recovering from illness of his daughter, Isabel. It is a fine example of Victorian Gothic architecture and still retains a primary school in part of the building.

Sir Alexander Fuller-Acland-Hood, c. 1906 (see also page 126). Sir A.A. Hood was the son of Sir Alexander Acland-Hood, 3rd Baronet, and his wife Isabel, daughter of Sir Peregrine Palmer Palmer-Fuller-Acland. He was born in Scotland in 1853 and was educated at Eton, Balliol College Oxford and Sandhurst. He was MP for Wellington from 1892 until 1911 and Vice-Chamberlain of the Household from 1900 to 1902, after which he was Parliamentary Secretary to the Treasury (Chief Whip) until 1905. He became a Privy Councillor in 1904 and Baron St Audries in 1911. The Hood family spawned several great naval leaders from around 1750 to 1820 and the battle cruiser Hood and her predecessors were named after them.

The entrance and drive to Quantock Lodge, *c.* 1904. Quantock Lodge is a vast and once-magnificent Gothic revival country house near Over Stowey. It was once occupied by the Stanley family who had succeeded to the Quantock estate through Mary Labouchère, who married Edward James Stanley. Mary died in 1920 and the lodge was bought by the council under the Public Health Act. Christies had sold the Stanleys' art collection in 1908.

Quantock Lodge, *c.* 1904. The house was started in 1857 and built in stages through the 1860s, mostly from local stone. A stable block was added in 1860 but was later partially demolished. In 1925 the house was opened as Quantock Lodge Sanatorium and remained as such until 1962. It was purchased by the headmaster of Cotham High School and remained in his ownership until 1998. Now again known as Quantock Lodge it is marketed as a centre for leisure, training courses, functions and house parties.

Crowcombe village, c. 1906. The earliest reference to the village dates to 854 where it was spelt Cerawicombe. The Domesday Book of 1086 has it listed as 'Crawcombe'. The church is dedicated to the Holy Ghost and dates to at least as far back as 1226. The oldest part of the church is the tower, which originally had an 80ft spire. This was struck by lightning and fell in 1724. The top of the spire was retained in a corner on the tower until its removal to the churchyard in 1954.

Crowcombe village and cross, c. 1906. In the distance is the Carew Arms Inn, originally the Lion or Three Lions, but renamed in 1814. Crowcombe once had a market and fair. The fourteenth-century cross marks the site on a triangle of grass. Like many villages in the area, population has declined. In 1831 it stood at 691 but had dropped to 405 by 1951. In 2002 population levels had risen again to 590. Crowcombe had a manor house as early as 1295 and the present Crowcombe Court was started in about 1723.

Alfoxton House, c. 1905. The house is in the parish of Stringston and William and Dorothy Wordsworth lived here between July 1797 and April 1798. Coleridge visited them here at the time. The present house was rebuilt in 1710 after a disastrous fire. It is now a hotel set in 50 acres of its own grounds. Also a hotel in the 1930s, it later became a boys' school then a Christian Holiday Home before reverting back to a hotel in 1958.

Aisholt, c. 1905. The little hamlet was much favoured by Coleridge, who wrote: 'the situation is delicious; all I could wish,' but Sara, his wife, preferred to live in a town. The village is still unspoilt and contains an old schoolhouse and church with a steep graveyard. Some of the woods contain ash and perhaps this is the origin of the village name. Above the village is a Devonian limestone outcrop and limekilns in which quarried limestone was burnt. A tiny cave in one of the quarries sometimes emits a strong draught, suggesting larger caverns somewhere beyond. Aisholt was a 'Thankful Village', having lost no residents in both world wars.

The Holford Beeches, c. 1906. The old gnarled beeches stand on a slope mounting to Longstone Hill. They were probably planted for shelter, ornament and timber, replacing the oaks that declined, due in part to the actions of local charcoal-burners. Now these trees are threatened by climate change as they do not favour hot, dry conditions.

Tannery Combe, c. 1906. This is often called Butterfly Combe, but is signposted from the village as Holford Combe. One of the cottages in the lower part of the combe used to belong to the village tanner. These buildings now comprise the Combe House Country Hotel. The iron waterwheel here is believed to be the largest in Somerset.

Hodder's Combe, Holford, c. 1906. Holford (the hollow field) lies below the spur of Hare Knap, a hill between Hodder's Combe and Tannery Combe. Three tributaries merge to form the stream in Hodder's Combe, and these rise below the high point on the western edge of the Quantocks – Bicknoller Post, Thorncombe Hill and Hurley Beacon.

Triscombe, c. 1906. The footpath up from Triscombe leads to the main Quantock ridge footpath from Lydeard Hill to West Quantoxhead. In the valley lies the huge Triscombe Quarry, now disused. Above here is Will's Neck (which means the ridge of the Welshman) which rises to 1,260ft. To the north lies Great Hill at 1,107ft. Back at the base of the valley nestles the little Blue Ball Inn just off the road around to Crowcombe.

Shepherds (Sheppard's) Combe, c. 1906. The zig-zag path down from Bicknoller Post to Holford will take you via Sheppard's Combe. This is the tranquil home of foxgloves, spindle-trees and hawthorns.

Holford Glen, c. 1906. This is one of the Quantocks' deepest combes. It starts at the confluence of the rivers that rise below Dowsborough Hill and Hurley Beacon. It is said a Huguenot silk factory once stood here. Wordsworth was inspired to write 'Lines Written in Early Spring' in Holford Glen. Montague Cooper also photographed the pretty little bridge here.

Adscombe Farm, c. 1906. The farm is situated in the valley below Quantock Lodge, a little way above the hamlet of Adscombe. A chapel was located near the farm and Coleridge refers to it in his 'Foster-Mother's Tale'.

Dodington Hall, c. 1905. The manor house stands on a raised terrace approached from the farmyard. The chimneypiece bears the date 1581 and the house is a fine example of Tudor workmanship. It is built from local Quantock red sandstone. In the early nineteenth century, the area was developed as a tin-mining centre, and an engine-house of Cornish design was built in the beech grove behind the hall. Another can be seen in a field to the east and both served the Buckingham Mine. Part of this extended to the beech grove where the miners discovered large natural caverns in the isolated limestone outcrop.

Cothelstone Tower, c. 1905. The tower was erected as a folly on Cothelstone Hill between 1768 and 1780 by Lady Hillsborough, the owner of the estate. Its prime purpose was for viewing the local countryside. The tower was destroyed around the end of the First World War and now only a pile of rubble remains. This, and an adjacent barrow or mound, are now scheduled monuments. Montague Cooper produced at least three views of the tower; two included the group of trees known as 'Seven Sisters'.

Quantock Staghounds, *c.* 1905. The pack was formed in 1902 by Mr E.V. Stanley of Quantock Lodge (*see* page 66). Mr Stanley joined the Devon and Somerset Staghounds in 1907 and the pack was disbanded in 1917, after which it was re-formed under Sir Denis Boles. The kennels are at West Bagborough.

Devon and Somerset Staghounds, *c.* 1905 (*see also* page 135). Although historically the wild red deer were hunted 'wherever found in Devon and Somerset', in practice the hunt operated between the River Taw in the west and the River Parrett in the east. Tiverton marked the southern boundary, while the Bristol Channel is to the north. Moorland and woodland within this area were the hunt's favourite haunts.

4
Burnham, Highbridge & District

Watchfield Windmill, Highbridge, c. 1905. This is a tower mill built of coursed lias stone with a slight convex batter. It is shown on a map of 1817 and was worked at the end of the nineteenth century by the Spearing family, who installed additional steam power in 1894. The mill was last worked in about 1918 and is now without its sails.

Highbridge from Bristol Bridge, *c.* 1906. Bristol Bridge, at 20.3ft above sea level, crosses the railway to the north-east of the town. St John's Church can be seen in this view. Highbridge stands at the mouth of the River Brue and was once an important centre of communications, with both the Great Western Railway and Somerset & Dorset railways having stations. In earlier times a canal took small cargo vessels as far as Glastonbury and there was a wharf on the river itself (*see* page 79).

Highbridge from the GWR station, *c.* 1906. At this time the town was also an important industrial centre but this has since declined. In 1933 Highbridge was sublimated within the joint town council district of Highbridge and Burnham-on-Sea. Before this the town's population was 2,585. This view shows the Cooper's Arms Hotel run in 1901 by Mrs Alice Card, a widow, and her son Robert.

Highbridge GWR station, *c.* 1906. The station was opened in 1841 by the Bristol & Exeter Railway on what is now the Great Western Main Line (the Great Western Railway took control of the station in 1876). An adjoining station was added by the Somerset Central Railway in 1854. This later became the Somerset & Dorset Joint Railway. The GWR station became Highbridge and Burnham-on-Sea station in 1962.

Somerset & Dorset Railway station, Highbridge, *c.* 1906. Also in this view can be seen the Somerset & Dorset's locomotive, carriage and wagon works. Somerset & Dorset coaching stock was built here from 1862 until 1913, the works eventually closing in 1930 with the loss of 300 jobs. The station had five platforms, and trains onward to Highbridge Wharf and Burnham-on-Sea had to cross the main GWR line at the northern end of the station. The station was closed to goods in 1964 and passengers in 1966.

The Highbridge rail crash, 20 June 1909. The accident occurred at 7.25 a.m. when a passenger train from Plymouth jumped a set of points, smashing into one of the coaches of a stationary goods train. Although there was much damage done to the passenger engine along with its newspaper van and first carriage, there was no loss of life as the train was only travelling at 25mph.

General Booth at Highbridge Town Hall, 20 August 1906. The photograph shows William Booth (with the white beard), the founder of the Salvation Army. Highbridge has a strong connection with the Salvation Army as Edward Higgins was born there in 1864. He became an officer in 1882 and travelled widely in the United States of America on Salvation Army business. Bramwell Booth succeeded his father, William, as General and appointed Edward Higgins as Chief of Staff in 1919. Bramwell Booth was forced to resign owing to ill health in 1929 and Edward Higgins became the Army's third General. The post returned to the Booth family in 1934 when Bramwell's sister, Evangeline, took command.

Highbridge Wharf, c. 1904. The wharf was at the western end of the Glastonbury Canal and was purchased by the Bristol & Exeter Railway in 1848. The wharf served the Somerset & Dorset shipping fleet and handled timber, bricks, steel rails, agricultural and dairy goods. Much of this travelled between Highbridge and South Wales for onward distribution by rail. The last Somerset & Dorset ship was sold in 1933 and the wharf eventually ceased business in 1964.

Esplanade and bandstand, Burnham-on-Sea, c. 1904. The bandstand was erected to commemorate the coronation of Edward VII. The bandstand's life was short as it was replaced by the pavilion in 1911.

Children's Special Service Mission (CSSM) at Burnham, *c.* 1908. This was the original name from 1867 of the organisation now called Scripture Union. The mission was started at Islington as a less formal version of Sunday School by Thomas Hughes and Josiah Spiers. Children were encouraged to bring their friends.

The Beach Mission at Burnham, *c.* 1908. This idea was popularised by the CSSM volunteers who set up large tents at popular seaside resorts typically for two or three weeks at a time. The missioners also lived in tents and used marquees for daytime and evening meetings. Sometimes a local church hall was also used. The Burnham Mission was organised by Mr Ashley King and his two sisters.

Waiting to start on Burnham Sands, c. 1904. Donkey rides have long been a feature on the sands at Burnham and Weston-super-Mare. The rides were introduced by the Victorians and the donkeys were led in a group at walking pace. Beaches were ideal because if a rider should fall off, they were less likely to hurt themselves on the sand.

The Esplanade from the sands, Burnham, c. 1904. The Esplanade was modified in about 1911 to give better protection in bad weather conditions. Many of the resort's best hotels were situated there. Also here was Beach Terrace, built mostly in the nineteenth century. Some of the properties were built for George Reed, Burnham's leading resident of the day.

The Esplanade, Burnham, on Regatta Day *c.* 1905. The Regatta is still held in Burnham but is now more focussed on the sailing. Events are still held on the beach and include a beach fun day, beach party and continental markets.

Regatta sports, Burnham, *c.* 1905. Early regattas were more focussed on sporting events which took place on the beach and attracted large crowds.

Burnham from the sea, c. 1906. This is the 19ft 6in *Gore*, a double-ended open boat known as a flatner. The vessels were constructed of tongue-and-grooved planks on a timber frame. Both inside and out were coated with tar. The two man crew are shown in this photograph. The one on the right has control of the rudder and mainsheet, while the other has charge of the jibsheet and dagger board. Vessels like this were built by H.J. Kimber of Highbridge and they were used for fishing in the river as well as estuary and coastal work.

The bandstand from the sands, c. 1906. The pavilion replaced this bandstand during redevelopment 1911–14. It now stands on the shortest pier in Britain (as originally built). It was the first concrete structure of its kind in Europe. Almost derelict by 1968, the pavilion has now been restored to its original condition.

A paddle-steamer at Burnham, c. 1905. The paddle-steamer sits alongside the jetty at the end of the Esplanade. P. and A. Campbell were the main operators in the Bristol Channel from the mid-nineteenth century to the late 1970s. The tradition is still continued by the last seagoing paddle-steamer in the world, P.S. *Waverley*.

Burnham beach, c. 1905. Burnham became Burnham-on-Sea in 1917 by sanction of the Somerset County Council. Between the wars a lot was done to enhance this situation. A marine lake was built at a cost of £10,000 but proved difficult to keep free of sand and silt. The children's paddling pool was gifted to the town in 1921 by Mr and Mrs J.B. Braithwaite, and a new promenade was constructed. Marine Cove with a goldfish pond was opened in 1927.

The beach at Burnham, c. 1905. Notice the beach huts for changing – although views of people in swimming attire are few. Beach attractions included swing-boats, merry-go-rounds, coconut shies and later Antonio's ice cream stall, popular after the First World War.

The Esplanade, Burnham, c. 1905. Burnham's growth in population nearly doubled in the years between 1891 and 1931. These years were really the heyday of the beach holiday in the United Kingdom. The Esplanade dates to earlier times, having been built in about 1796.

A rough sea at Burnham, c. 1905. Residents of the Bristol Channel coast are well used to bad sea conditions. None were as bad as the great flood of 1607, which killed thousands of people. Latest research suggests that the cause may have been a tsunami. The stone wall of the Esplanade was replaced with a new sea wall, designed to restrict damage from rough seas.

Coronation procession, 1911. Burnham really went to town on 22 July 1911 for the Coronation of King George V. This view shows Victoria Street with Berrills hairdressers and tobacconists and Wells Brothers' butchers. Much of the town was decorated. High arches were built in Oxford Street and Abingdon Street proclaiming 'Long Live the King'.

Burnham-on-Sea lifeboat, c. 1905. The first lifeboat was presented to the Corporation of Bridgwater by Sir Peregrine Acland after a local shipping disaster. In 1847 a new ten-oared boat replaced the old one, having been built by Gale of Whitby. The Royal National Lifeboat Institution (RNLI) took over the lifeboat station in 1866 and accepted a 32ft ten-oared boat donated by the town of Cheltenham. In 1874 a new lifeboat station was built next to the railway station.

Coronation procession, 1911 (*see also* page 86). Victoria Street is in the background of this photograph. In 1887 the lifeboat *John Godfrey* Morris replaced the *Cheltenham*, but this view shows the *Philip Beach*, a 32ft boat acquired in 1902. In 1930 motor lifeboats replaced those at Minehead and Weston-super-Mare and the Burnham station closed. Service was resumed by an independent charity, Burnham Area Rescue Boat (BARB), in 1994. In 2003 the RNLI took over from BARB at their request.

Burnham Amateur Swimming Club, 1908. There were plenty of sporting activities in Burnham around this time, as many old postcards show. These included bowls, golf, sand yachting, sailing, cricket, angling, walking, cycling, football, rugby and even dancing in the Manor Gardens in the 1920s.

Burnham Town Hockey Club, 1908/9. Seen here are, back row, left to right: W.H.C. Stiling, P.J. Deaken, W. Pulsford-Lang, J. Lewis, A.T. Tyler, G. Hauser, the Revd H.J. Ker Thompson MA, JP. Front row: J. Rowley, P.F. Bean, W. Halse-Tucker (secretary), N.J. Petheram (captain), S. Wyatt, P. Thomas, F.D. Churchill.

Coronation procession prize winner, 22 June 1911. A procession was included in the coronation celebrations. This prize-winning entry was a decorated baker's cart, entered by the Victoria Café. The company had premises at 17 Victoria Street and was owned by the Weare family.

La Retraite, Burnham. The sender of this postcard states, 'The Convent is very nice indeed. There are large and lovely gardens, several fields where we may go every day. We are here with English young ladies.' La Retraite (The Retreat) began in seventeenth-century Brittany to sustain people suffering materially and spiritually. The first retreat house was opened for men in Vannes in 1663. The Burnham Retreat was known as the Convent of the Retreat of the Sacred Heart of Jesus. It contained a boarding school and was housed in The Rookery.

The River, Burnham, *c.* 1905. The River Brue did not run through Burnham but entered the sea at the end of the South Esplanade. The river passed through Highbridge via an artificial cut, with Highbridge Wharf to the north being the original route. There were various brickworks to the north while South Highbridge and Alstone lay on the other side.

The golf links, *c.* 1905. Burnham and Berrow golf course was laid out by Charles Gibson of Westward Ho! in 1890. Originally a nine-hole course, it became a full eighteen-hole course in 1897. J.H. Taylor became the club's first professional in 1891 but left the club eighteen months later.

A general view of Burnham from the lighthouse, c. 1905. Burnham had two lighthouses, both working in conjunction with one another. The low lighthouse was a wooden structure on legs built in 1832. The high lighthouse, a more traditional design, was also built the same year. This view is from the 120ft high lighthouse.

Rocks at Brean Down, c. 1905. At this time the coast from Burnham to Brean Down was completely undeveloped. It was a quiet spot even after the Second World War and it was still possible to park on the beach in relative solitude. Now the area is jam-packed with holiday resorts and caravan parks. The mile-long walk along Brean Down takes you to the old fortification at the end which was completed in 1870. In 1900 a huge explosion occurred at the fort when a soldier fired his gun into one of the magazines.

Mark Causeway, *c.* 1906. Mark Causeway was transferred to Mark from East Brent in 1885. It is one of the longest villages in Somerset and at this time was primarily a farming community. Listed in directories were a shoemaker, an iron and brass foundry, a butcher, a post office (which was also a draper and grocer) and a cooper.

The Crossways, East Brent, *c.* 1906. This view shows Alfred Emery's Brent Knoll Inn. He ran this hostelry with his wife, Elizabeth, assisted by her father, brother and sister. The war memorial was erected opposite the inn on the junction of the A370 and the Old Bristol Road in 1921. The stonemason was Mr Emery of Burnham-on-Sea.

Brent Knoll, c. 1905. Brent Knoll is 450ft high and is an outcrop of clay and limestone which dates from the Jurassic period. Bronze Age and Iron Age people inhabited the summit. The church is dedicated to St Michael and has a Norman doorway, and the present nave was built in 1290. In about 1880 the village changed its name from South Brent to Brent Knoll to avoid confusion with South Brent in Devon.

Huntspill and Ilex Stores, c. 1905. Mr Cooper produced this card for Gilbert Burnett, the owner of Ilex Stores. On the back is written, 'Hope to call upon you on or about Mon 5th Sept. when your commands will be esteemed and receive prompt attention.' Gilbert Burnett was born in Huntspill in about 1870 and lived with his wife Annie. The couple employed one servant. The 1901 Census describes Gilbert as a draper, grocer and general shopkeeper and his stores, dating from 1792, took its name from an Ilex tree in the garden. The premises are now Ilex Court.

Family group cabinet card, c. 1906. This was issued before the Chard branch opened around 1908. Cabinet cards and the smaller cartes de visite were produced by most local photographers from the 1850s until about 1910. They are rarely captioned as they were saved in special albums where captions could be added. They are, however, a good example of the photographer's studio work and provide much information on fashions at the time.

5

Minehead & North Somerset

Montague Cooper cabinet card, *c.* 1895. This unusual card shows a sailor between the wheel and binnacle on a sailing ship somewhere in North Somerset. The wheel is unusual because it has a rudder indicator showing degrees of steering to port and starboard. On older vessels it was normal just to have one of the wheel handles capped with brass. This, in the uppermost position, told the helmsman that the rudder was set straight ahead. The steering position and binnacle was at the stern on many sailing ships.

Minehead, the bay and North Hill, *c.* 1904. In 1087 the Manor of Minehead had a population of sixty-nine. Like several seaside towns in Somerset it developed into a popular resort during the nineteenth century and by 1901 had a population of 2,511. Numerous fine hotels were built and a pier was added in 1901 by the Campbell Steamboat Company. The pier was 700ft long but unfortunately it was removed during the Second World War as it was in the way of a gun emplacement.

Bird's-eye view towards Dunster, *c.* 1904. During the sixteenth century all the flat land was sea. It came up to Conygar Hill and Dunster had a harbour. Much of the seaward side is now the Butlins holiday camp. Smoke can be seen rising from Minehead station. The railway came in 1874 and British Railways closed the line in 1971. The whole line back to Bishops Lydeard is now run by the West Somerset Railway.

A panorama of the sea front, Minehead, c. 1904. Like Burnham-on-Sea, Minehead developed rapidly in Victorian times. Sadly it lacked the sandy beach that Burnham had and never achieved the popularity of either Burnham or Weston-super-Mare. When the pier closed Minehead went into decline but was revived by the opening of Butlins holiday camp and the West Somerset Railway.

Market House and Square, Minehead, c. 1904. This new building was erected in 1902 to replace the smaller one, then known as the Fish Market.

Market House and the Avenue, Minehead, c. 1904. The Avenue was a fine Victorian street with trees planted along both sides. It has appeared in many postcards of Minehead including those dating from 1965, which still show the trees, though far fewer in number than in the early views.

The Avenue from the sea, c. 1904. Originally an open stream ran down the Avenue but it has been covered over for many years. Nowadays the Avenue is the very heart of Minehead leading from the town centre right down to the sea front.

The Esplanade, Minehead, *c.* 1904. Montague Cooper produced this postcard for Cox, Sons & Company, stationers at Park Street. The Esplanade is now home to various hotels and guesthouses. The Jubilee Gardens are also situated here with its popular snack bar. Beyond the Esplanade is the now redeveloped area of Quay Street, leading to the harbour.

Hopcott Hotel, *c.* 1904. In this photograph the grass outside the hotel is being cut. The Hopcott was one of several good private hotels around Minehead at this time. Others included the Plume of Feathers, the Carlton, the Beach Hotel (built to coincide with the coming of the railway) and the magnificent Metropole Hotel which stood in 4 acres of grounds. The Metropole had croquet and tennis lawns and was often used by the Indian Rajahs.

Bentfield Hucks at Minehead in 1911. The aircraft was one of two Blackburn Mercurys that were entered in the 1911 *Daily Mail* Circuit of Britain. One crashed on take-off and this machine, piloted by Hucks, did not complete the first stage. It was converted to a two-seater and then used for a tour of the West Country. Hucks was the first English pilot to loop an aeroplane in 1913. He served in the BEF early in the First World War, but was invalided out with pleurisy in 1915. Hucks died on 7 November 1918 from Spanish 'flu at the age of thirty-five.

Blenheim Road, Minehead, *c.* 1906. The map of 1890 shows only five properties here at the south end of the road. Further development in the fields south of Quay Lane resulted in the west side of the street being completed by around 1906. At this time only fields existed to the east. The famous author Arthur C. Clarke was born at 13 Blenheim Road in December 1917.

Quay Street, Minehead, *c.* 1905. This charming little scene no longer exists. The houses to the seaward side of Quay Street were removed after the great storm of 1911. Originally there was a wooden jetty before the harbour was built. It stood near Lamb Cottage which was also demolished in about 1911.

The Old Town and Harbour, Minehead, *c.* 1905. A disastrous fire in 1791 burnt down much of Quay Town and Middle Town. The fire originated in the premises of Edward May, a miller who was experimenting with the burning of a tar barrel. The wind blew the flames onto a stack of furze in his yard and the blaze quickly spread, destroying around eighty houses.

The Quay, *c.* 1905. The Luttrells provided the town with a stone harbour, which was completed in 1616. It was enlarged to a length of 700ft in 1901, the same year that the pier was built. The following year a new lifeboat station was built. It seems the demolition of the pier in 1940 was unnecessary; the guns shook the harbour wall so much that it was not possible to use them. The harbour was eventually sold by Squire Luttrell to Minehead Council in 1951.

Hotel Metropole, *c.* 1903. Montague Cooper's two-seater De Dion car, registered in 1903, is outside.

The Plume of Feathers Hotel, *c.* 1904. Mr Cooper's car again stands outside. This lovely old coaching inn stood in Wellington Square. It was demolished in 1965 to build a modern block of shops. Its claim to fame is that Daniel Defoe stayed here in 1772. The inn name was transferred to the Carlton Hotel as the Carlton Plume of Feathers. This too has been demolished and in 2003 new retirement flats were built on the site.

The Parks and Hill, Minehead, *c.* 1904. There are two ancient farms on the upper parts of the hill. These are known as East Myne and West Myne. A number of fine Georgian town houses were built at the Parks and this is now a favoured residential spot at Minehead.

The parish church and Ancient Steps, *c.* 1904. In the fifteenth century there were three main towns comprising Minehead: Middle Town was around the Priory, Quay Town beside the sea and this area, near the church, was known as Higher Town. The church is dedicated to St Andrew.

East Quantoxhead Village, *c.* 1904. The parish and village of East Quantoxhead is 4 miles east of Williton station, lying just off the main A39. Around this time the village was a thriving community with shops, school and an inn. The inn closed in 1916 and is now known as Prospect House. The population of the village declined from 339 in 1861 to around 100 in more recent times.

East Quantoxhead showing the duck pond, *c.* 1904. The pond is close to the Court House, an Elizabethan manor. It was constructed to hold water for a mill. Close by are some fine medieval barns which have now been restored. The Court House was established by Sir Hugh Lutterell, who died in 1522 and is buried in the little church close by. The house still remains in the Lutterell family.

Porlock Weir, *c.* 1913. This little port a mile west of Porlock village once played a major part in the commercial life of this area of Exmoor. With difficult routes by land, a route by sea was often the easiest way to and from the area. With a tidal range of about 29ft, the lock gates were built in 1913 to enclose the harbour. They are now used mainly to flush pebbles from the harbour.

Porlock Weir, *c.* 1905. Culbone Woods, close to Porlock Weir, was once the site of a charcoal-burning industry. Stone ruins and trackways can still be traced in the woods. Oaks were also felled for the shipbuilding industry and some of the saw pits are still visible. Until about 1910, a large group of feral goats lived in the area and their milk, skins and meat was traded at Porlock Weir. The little port remains one of the best-preserved haven harbours in England.

The stagecoach on Porlock Hill, c. 1905. This coach ran from Minehead to Lynton until 1920, when it was replaced by motor coaches. The Victorians had popularised Lynton and Lynmouth, calling them the 'little Switzerland of England'. The hill, which at one place has a gradient of 1:4, was first ascended by a motor car in 1900 for a bet. Today the toll road can be used. It is a leisurely 1:14 and 1 mile longer.

The Ship Inn, Porlock. The Ship Inn was built in 1290, making it one of the oldest inns in the country. Centuries ago the sea came very close to the inn, making it an ideal spot for smugglers. Until the mid-nineteenth century, visitors would have arrived on foot or on horseback. In 1843 the first stagecoach arrived drawing out the locals in scores to view it. The toll road was built in 1840 and in the early days the tolls were collected by the inn staff. When the stagecoach route was established, an extra two horses were stabled at the inn to assist in the long climb up the hill.

Porlock village, *c.* 1905. In 1887 Porlock parish was described as being of 6,019 acres, and having a population of 765. The village itself is 6 miles west of Minehead. In 2002 the village had a population of 1,377. It was referred to by Coleridge when a 'person from Porlock' interrupted him during the composition of his poem 'Kubla Khan'.

Allerford, *c.* 1905. Like the Ship Inn at Porlock and Selworthy Forge, this is a view often sold on postcards by various photographers. Mr Cooper has taken the standard view showing the medieval packhorse bridge spanning Aller Water, a tributary of Horner Water. The bridge is a more unusual two-arch structure. Allerford is situated 2 miles west of Minehead.

Walnut Tree and Cottage, Bossington, *c.* 1905. Bossington is a hamlet lying 1 mile from Porlock under Bossington Beacon, the west end of North Hill. The area lies within the National Trust's Holnicote Estate. On Bossington Beach are the remains of a lime kiln. Lime was traditionally brought in by boat and heated to render it usable for addition to the local acidic soil.

Bird's-eye view of Williton, c. 1906. Williton is a small town 2 miles south of Watchet. It is one of the ten stations on the West Somerset Railway. The station was built in 1862. The name of Williton is Anglo-Saxon and means 'estate on the River Willet'. St Peter's church in Bridge Street was originally a dependant chapel of St Decumans and dedicated to All Saints. It was largely rebuilt in the nineteenth century. The town has had its own newspaper, the *West Somerset Free Press*, since 1860.

Williton Schools, c. 1906. The building was erected in 1871/2 with a masters' house at a cost of £1,400 for 200 children. The average attendance at this time was 170 and Trethern Jose Gard was the headmaster. In February 1996, St Peter's Church of England School moved to a new site in the grounds of Danesfield and the old school was converted to social housing for the community.

Williton, Stream Farm, c. 1906. Stream Farm nestles in the valley below Orchard Wyndham House. There were two farms here, one at Higher Stream and the other at Lower Stream. This appears to be Higher Stream, owned at this time by Alfred Date and his family. John Harris Haddon owned Lower Stream Farm and both men were born locally.

Dunster village and yarn market, c. 1906. This is a classic Somerset view photographed by many postcard publishers. The yarn market was built in 1609 as Dunster was an important cloth-making centre. Market day was the biggest event for miles around. Dunster has a beach about half a mile south of the village centre and a station on the West Somerset Railway.

Castle and Grabhurst, *c.* 1906. Until the reign of Elizabeth I, Dunster was a busy port known as Dunster Haven. All the flat land below the castle was originally below sea level. The castle site dates back to Norman times and a thirteenth-century gatehouse survives. The present building was remodelled between 1868 and 1872 by Antony Salvin for the Luttrell family and is open to the public. Much work was carried out on the roof in 2007.

Dunkery from Wheddon Cross, *c.* 1906. This photograph gives a view of the southern slope of Dunkery Hill above Bin Combe and Mansley Combe. The road from Wheddon Cross passes the head of Mansley Combe through Dunkery Gate and then skirts the highest point in Somerset, the 1,705ft Dunkery Beacon, to drop down again to Luccombe.

Wheddon Cross, c. 1906. Wheddon Cross and Cutcombe are now, in effect, a single large village in the centre of Exmoor National Park. They are the highest villages in Exmoor and are situated on the crossroads of the main routes between Minehead and Dulverton (north–south) and Taunton to North Devon (east–west).

The school at Wheddon Cross, c. 1906. Now known as Cutcombe Church of England First School, it was established in 1876 with money from a trust from the will of Richard Elsworth. The school and master's house were erected in 1875 for 200 children; however, average attendance in 1902 was only fifty-nine. The master was Henry C. Hayes.

Timberscombe village and church, c. 1906. The church here was originally dedicated to St Michael and All Angels. The main body of the church dates from the fifteenth century, but the tower was rebuilt in 1714 at the expense of Richard Elsworth Esq. The church is now dedicated to St Petroc, the sixth-century Celtic missionary from Wales. The church has a Tudor rood screen.

A bird's-eye view of Timberscombe, c. 1906. The village lies in a valley 2½ miles south-west of Dunster. It was situated on the turnpike road from Dunster to Dulverton. Near the church are the Lion Inn, built in about 1600, and the sixteenth-century Great House. The directory for 1910 lists 138 residents, most of them being involved in agriculture and included a timber haulier, carpenter, saddler, grocer and draper, blacksmith and gamekeeper. Mrs M. Lyddon was the postmistress and Samuel Stenner ran the Lion Inn together with a butcher's shop.

Kilve village, c. 1906. Kilve lies on the A39 midway between Bridgwater and Minehead. This view shows the Hood Arms Hotel, a seventeenth-century coaching inn. The brewery firm of Starkey, Knight and Ford owned the premises at this time. The landlord was the appropriately named Amos Wine, formerly a carpenter from Bicknoller. The lane next to the inn leads down to Kilve beach, where the remains of an oil-shale extraction plant can be seen. This was installed in the 1920s but the business soon became defunct.

West Somerset Foxhounds at St Audries, c. 1909. At this time the Hon. Secretary of the Hunt was Henry T. Daniel. In 1909 a special testimonial was held for Jack Burge, the First Whip, who was leaving after twenty-eight years' service. Until 1946 the hunt's country was much larger but then it was divided between the West Somerset (Western Farmers) and the West Somerset (Quantock Farmers). In 1954 the two hunts became completely independent. The Western Farmers retained the original name and the Quantock farmers became the West Somerset Vale Hunt.

St Audries Bay, c. 1906. The bay is situated between Watchet and East Quantoxhead. This area of coastline is much favoured by fossil collectors. Fossils from the Jurassic period (some 200 million years ago) are to be found there, and there are fine examples of lower lias pavements on the foreshore.

St Audries House, c. 1906. The house and estate lies close to St Audries Bay and was the home of the Malets during the seventeenth and eighteenth centuries, and later belonged to the Hood and Acland families, both related to the Malets (*see* pages 65 and 126). Huge alterations were carried out by Sir Peregrine Acland after he bought the estate in 1835. He also removed buildings at West Quantoxhead to improve the view. Later the estate was broken up and in 1934 the house and grounds were sold and became a school for girls. It was used as a Buddhist retreat in 2000, but today serves as an exclusive wedding venue.

Selworthy Forge, *c.* 1904. The village is part of the National Trust's huge Holnicote Estate. This consists of over 12,000 acres of Exmoor coast and countryside. The smithy was at Buddle Hill just to the south-west of Selworthy and nearby were kennels and saw mills. George Maine was the owner of the Forge in 1910.

Raleigh Cottage, Cutcombe, *c.* 1904. The cottage sits above the valley running down the flank of Dunkery Hill to Wheddon Cross and Cutcombe. In the early twentieth century it was home to widower James Coles, who was still working as a road contractor in his mid-seventies. Many able-bodied working-class men worked until they died at this time. James's widowed sister-in-law lived-in as his housekeeper. The cottage used to be a shooting-box for Lord of the Manor, the Hon. P.P. Bouverie.

Cutcombe village, c. 1906. Cutcombe is 5 miles from Dunster and 8 miles from Dulverton. It is situated on Cutcombe Ford under Dunkery Beacon. The church in Early English style is dedicated to St John.

Wootton Courtenay, c. 1906. Spellings for the name vary but in the Domesday Book the village was originally Otone, meaning settlement by the wood. The Courtenay part was added in the thirteenth century when the Courtenay family became owners of the manor. The main village lies beneath the hillside of Wootton Common and the parish contains the hamlets of Huntscott, Brockwell and Ford.

Wootton Courtenay, c. 1905. This postcard was produced by Mr Cooper for George Burnell, the postmaster. By 1902 George Burnell seems to have built up quite a little empire at Wootton Courtenay. As well as postmaster, he was also a grocer, draper, tailor, outfitter and general commission agent. The Burnell Brothers also ran the local bakery.

Wootton Courtenay, c. 1905. 'Burnell' is marked on the wall. George's wife, Mary, ran Fernlea, offering apartments and refreshments for tourists and visitors to Exmoor, while George arranged for carriages to be hired. George was a local man, born in about 1845. His wife Mary came from Wellington and was eleven years his junior. Together they employed four servants to assist in their businesses.

A bird's-eye view of Stogumber, *c.* 1906. Mr Cooper produced this card for Frederick Inkpen, a grocer and draper in Stogumber. The village lies in a valley between the Quantocks and the Brendons at a stream crossing. It was once described as a small market town and a brewery was established here in about 1840. This was begun by G. Elers, but became Sloman and Brander in about 1880. The final owner was Mathew Mossman, who was at the brewery from about 1904 until 1910. The water from the brewery came from a spring known as Harry Hill's Well.

Hill Street, Stogumber, *c.* 1906. Today the village is a much quieter place. In 1851 the population was nearly 1,500, but this has declined to around 600 today. Hill Street leads to High Street and the White Horse Inn, a shop and the red sandstone church – St Mary's. The village had a station on the Taunton to Minehead line, but it was not close enough to have a major impact on the village's commercial life.

6
Wellington, Wiveliscombe, Milverton & District

A cabinet card, *c.* 1907. This card was produced before the Chard branch opened in about 1909.

Harding Butchers, *c.* 1910. Tom Harold Harding opened a butcher's shop at 43 Mantle Street in about 1908. This later changed to 82a Mantle Street, Wellington. There were nearly 500 butcher's shops in Somerset in 1902.

Walter Lane, Butcher, *c.* 1910. This shop was at 29 High Street. In this view we see heifers, left and right, with a fat hog and fat pig. The family lived at the shop and Walter employed his brother-in-law, Robert Trenchard, and young Henry Crabb, a servant and butcher's help. Walter lived with his wife, Anna, and two sons, John and Ernest.

Two postcards commissioned by shop owners, c. 1910. G. Forsyth was a draper and milliner at 25 Fore Street, Wellington. The shoe shop was one of a chain owned by Frisby's. This one was at 3 High Street, Wellington. Like the previous two views, the postcards were commissioned as advertisements and a means of communication to customers. Multiple deliveries by mail on a daily basis and cheap postal rates made this method of communication very effective. They are rarely captioned, so a great deal of detective work is required to identify the addresses. It usually helps if they are postmarked. Few of these types of postcards were kept by recipients, so they are very collectable. Most show an aspect of social history far removed from today's chain stores and supermarkets.

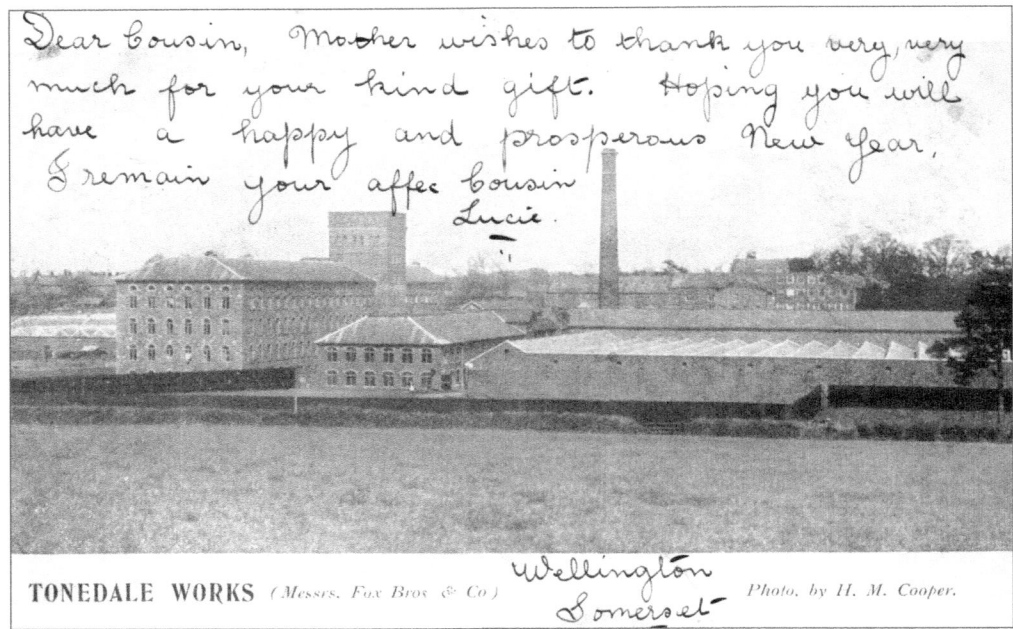

Tonedale Works. An early undivided back card, postmarked 1903. Only a handful of Cooper cards are known from this date. This woollen factory was built by Thomas Fox between 1801 and 1803 on the site of the town's flour mill. The factory was reconstructed after a fire in 1821 and steam power was installed in 1840. Together with the Elworthy family, who ran further woollen mills at Westford, Fox's was the town's principal employer throughout the nineteenth century.

A procession at Wellington, c. 1911. This would appear to be the 1911 Coronation, an event well photographed by Mr Cooper. 1911 was an exciting year for Wellingtonians as 200 people camped out to see the aviators in the Daily Mail Air Race. This card was not posted until 1961!

Wellington High Street, *c.* 1910. This view shows the London Central Meat Company at no. 30, J. Davey and Sons corn stores and Sidney Harold Hodges, tailor and costumier, at no. 22.

Wellington High Street, *c.* 1909. Scott Hammett's shoe shop is in the background of this photograph. Frederick Scott Hammett (1847–1904) introduced the telephone to Wellington and died aged fifty-seven. His wife committed suicide two years later. The shoe and boot business was run by their eldest son, Charles, until 1928. Wellington's first motor works were opened at 9 High Street in 1903 by J.M. Richardson of Coventry.

The Committee Rooms of Sir Alexander Fuller Acland-Hood at Wellington, 1906. Sir Alec was returned to Parliament in this election with a majority of 272. He was MP for Wellington from 1892 until 1911, after which he was ennobled as Baron St Audries. He died in June 1917, aged sixty-three, and was succeeded in his titles by his eldest son, Alexander.

The town centre, Wellington, c. 1907. This postcard was sent to Russia in 1908. The town hall was built in 1833 and originally measured 25ft by 45ft. It was enlarged in 1896 and housed Wellington's first cinema, being officially licensed as such in 1909. The building continued to house a cinema, eventually becoming the Tivoli and later the Rex, which came into competition with the purpose-built Wellesley Cinema in 1937. The Rex closed shortly after the Second World War.

Wellington Town Hall and post office, *c.* 1909. The White Hart Inn was the home to an early Wellington post office. Two addresses in High Street housed the post office in the 1830s and 1840s and it moved to Fore Street in 1871. In 1885 the business transferred to the former Market House Inn above. In 1911 the post office then returned to the remodernised White Hart Inn building.

Waterloo Road, *c.* 1909. The name denotes the connection with the town and the Duke of Wellington. On the right is the Dolphin Inn, run by widow Sarah Fursdon in 1901, with a little help from her aged mother, Harriet Warren, and Ellen Alderman, a young servant. The notice on the wall points to Grafton's Aerated Water Works, originally in the High Street but at Waterloo Road from about 1905 to 1935. The company also had a branch at Exeter and were well known for their ginger beer in stoneware bottles.

Bovet Street, *c.* 1905. As with Taunton, it seems likely that Mr Cooper produced postcards of many of Wellington's side-streets. Bovet Street appears to have been built in the 1890s as it is not listed on the 1891 Census. Bovet is a local family name: a Philip Bovet of Wellington and Colonel Richard Bovet, Commander of Monmouth's Blue Regiment, were executed for their part in Monmouth's Rebellion of 1685. Another Richard Bovet built Swan House (later Clifford House) in Wellington in 1770.

Springfield, Wellington, *c.* 1905. A less than enthusiastic bunch of children stand in the narrow road at Springfield. The first of these terraced houses was built in 1883.

Flax workers' camp in the cricket field, 1918. The crop is sown in early spring and can be harvested in midsummer. The mature yellow stems are pulled by hand and stacked in bundles. The stems are then walked repeatedly or beaten with flail to remove the seed bolls. More commonly the top end of the stems were pulled through a comb-like tool called a ripple. The stems were then retted by leaving them exposed to the weather or soaking for several weeks. Scutching came next, which loosened and crushed the stems to produce the long fibres needed for linen manufacture. About two-thirds of the stems were good for this.

Victoria Terrace at Rockwell Green, c. 1908. Just beyond the terrace is Westford Bridge under which the locomotive *City of Truro* is supposed to have achieved over 100mph in May 1904. The official 100mph limit was exceeded thirty years later by the *Flying Scotsman*. *City of Truro's* timed 102.3mph has been thrown into doubt as there was no secondary time-keeper. Modern students of locomotive performance doubt that *City of Truro* could have developed sufficient horsepower to exceed 95mph. Nevertheless, thousands of people visited this section of track exactly 100 years later when a restored *City of Truro* repeated its famous journey.

Two views of Rockwell Green. In the distance in the photograph above is All Saints' Church, which was built in 1889 on land given by Samuel Dobree, and local industrialist Frederick Thomas Elworthy provided financial support. The original church had no spire, but one was added in 1907 – quite rare for Somerset. The peal of six bells was installed in 1909. The brick water tower can also be seen here. Water came from springs near Westford and was pumped to the tower from a pumping station powered by gas engines. A larger concrete tower was built next to the brick tower in 1935.

Rockwell Green, c. 1908. Perhaps these children are on their way to school – the tall building on the left. Robert Jarratt, vicar of Wellington, paid for the building in 1841 and it was enlarged in 1892; by 1906 it accommodated 180 boys and girls and eighty infants. The school moved to Brooklands Road in 1972 and Rockwell Green village hall opened here in 1977. The long terrace of houses is not on the 1891 map, so must have been completed in about 1900. At the end of the terrace is the Baptist Chapel erected in 1860 and restored in 1903/4 when an adjoining school was added. Rockwell Green's population in 1901 was 1,573.

Milverton station, c. 1915. Work on the railway from Norton Fitzwarren to Wiveliscombe started shortly after the Devon & Somerset Railway Act of 1864. Excavations commenced at Ford Bridge in October 1865. The first train carrying directors and shareholders ran through Milverton on 21 February 1871 and the boys from the local school were allowed out to see it. The official opening of the line to Wiveliscombe took place on 8 June 1871 and was marked by a general holiday. By late July 1871 regular cheap excursions to Weston-super-Mare were on offer. The line from Norton to Milverton was doubled in 1937, mostly as a result of Ilfracombe excursion traffic. Like many other branch lines, the system closed in the mid-1960s.

The birthplace of Dr Thomas Young, Milverton. This English physician and physicist was born in Milverton on 13 June 1773 and died in London on 10 May 1829. Thomas Young was extensively educated and an expert in many fields. As an Egyptologist he helped decipher the Rosetta Stone and he also studied physiological optics and the nature of light. He became a scientific adviser to the Admiralty and gave many lectures at the Royal Institution on acoustics, optics, gravitation, astronomy, tides, electricity, climate and many other subjects.

Council Schools, Milverton, c. 1907. The school opened in 1835, having been built at a cost of £765, a third of which was donated by Lambe's Charity. The Education Act of 1902 abolished local school boards and the Milverton school was transferred to the County Council, who agreed to pay all rates, taxes and other outgoings. The school became a primary school in 1953 when the older pupils transferred to Wiveliscombe Comprehensive School.

Wiveliscombe from the railway. The railway arrived in 1871 and at this time the town was a significant borough, market and cloth town. It was also home to a large brewery belonging to the Hancock family. The company became Arnold & Hancock Ltd in 1927. The author spent many happy hours digging out old stone ginger beer bottles from the brewery tip many years ago. The population of Wiveliscombe is now is less than 3,000 but a survey in 1997 revealed that there were over 300 businesses within 5 miles of the town.

The market place and town hall, Wiveliscombe, c. 1906. The town hall was designed by Richard Carver and erected by Alexander Baring, MP for Taunton from 1806 to 1826. The building opened on 3 August 1842 and has always remained in private ownership. It was bought for £1,100 by local corn factor John Merchant in 1894. After the First World War the Cooperative Society acquired the building, which they opened as a store in 1921. The portico and balcony were removed and replaced by a continuous shop front for the Co-op and G. Small & Sons Ltd. The clock belongs to the council.

Abbotsfield House, Wiveliscombe, c. 1905. The house was built in 1875 for Charles Lukey Collard. The 50-acre site was purchased by Collard in 1870 from Samuel Lutley. The London building firm used local red sandstone with white limestone dressings. The roof slates were quarried at Okehampton. William Macadam Smith JP bought the property in 1896 for £10,040 and was in residence at the time of the 1901 Census with his wife, Helena, and two daughters. They employed a housekeeper, a housemaid, a scullery maid, a kitchen maid and a footman.

The White Horse Hotel and bridge, Exford, c. 1905. The bridge was rebuilt in 1930 on a medieval site. It is a three-arch span with semi-circular headed arches. The village church of St Mary dates to the fifteenth century and is about half a mile from the village itself.

The Devon and Somerset Staghounds at Exford Kennels, c. 1905. These were built by Montague Bissett in 1875 and are still in use. Exford is popular for horse riding, shooting and fishing and is situated at the very heart of the Exmoor National Park.

At Exford Bridge, c. 1905. The sign states 'Smith, Saddle and Harness Maker'. Exford is a very rural parish which had a population of 429 in 2001; a decrease of 4 per cent since the 1991 Census. There are currently 175 occupied households. Hunting on Exmoor dates back to the time of Queen Elizabeth I, when the area was hunted as a Royal Forest. The Devon and Somerset pack has been recorded since 1775, a notable master being Mr Fenwick Bisset, who held the post for over twenty-five years.

The Crown Hotel, Exford, *c.* 1906. Ethel Amery, a widow, ran the hotel in 1901 but by this time the name of J.H. Tarr appears on the building. The Exmoor Stores, with their delivery van outside, was owned by Walter E. Batchelor, a native of Rotherhithe. He lived with his wife, Annie, and young son, Leslie. They were sufficiently well-off to be able to afford a servant/domestic nurse. The car, again, probably belonged to Mr Cooper.

Dulverton – a bird's-eye view, *c.* 1906. The town can trace its history back to Saxon times and is mentioned in the Domesday Book of 1086. Dulverton is the southern gateway to Exmoor and retains much of its old-world charm. The town's 1,300-strong population remains very much the same as it did 100 years ago.

Dulverton, the Cottage and Mount, *c.* 1905. This view shows the west side of the Barle Valley. The Mount is situated on the top right of the photograph on a raised position above Barle Bridge. The Cottage is top left, next to the Mossy Park Plantation. It has been a landmark since the early nineteenth century and was built for the Fry family of chocolate fame. A Mr Abbott was in residence at the time of this photograph.

Dulverton Weir from Northmoor Road, *c.* 1905. In the distance is Weir Head and Weirhead Cottages. Northmoor Road runs along the River Barle and is a key link between Dulverton and other parts of Exmoor National Park. The river wall was rebuilt in a major scheme during 2007.

Ashbrittle, the village, c. 1906. Ashbrittle is a village and parish 6 miles west of Wellington. The population of the parish in 1901 was 325. Nearly all the trades here at that time were connected with agriculture. James Lamprey ran a Temperance Hotel in the village in the early twentieth century.

Ashbrittle, the mansion, c. 1906. At this time, this fine property was owned by Sir John Henry Priestly Churchill Edwards, 3rd Baronet (1889–1942). By 1910 the Revd Julian Cunningham, Curate in Charge, lived here having moved from Liverpool. He was educated in Ireland and moved to Ashbrittle in 1904.

Kyrle House, Ashbrittle, and surrounding countryside, c. 1904. This was home to John E. Clark who described his occupation in 1901 as 'living on own means'. He was not a local man, having been born in Yorkshire in about 1860. He employed two servants – a cook and housemaid.

Ashbrittle Church, c. 1904. The churchyard is famous for its 3,000-year-old yew tree. This has a girth of 40ft and a vast canopy resulting from regeneration over the centuries. The church is dedicated to St John the Baptist and is principally of Perpendicular style. Many portions of the building were rebuilt and restored in the nineteenth century when the original building fell into disrepair.

The Royal Oak Inn, Winsford, *c.* 1905. For some reason Mr Cooper has deleted the writing on the pub sign. Originally the building was a twelfth-century farmhouse and dairy. It is still an important base for people who wish to explore the Exmoor National Park.

Winsford Village, *c.* 1905. The writer of this card states this to be 'the prettiest village in England'. Winsford is a village and parish 5 miles north-west of Dulverton and 14 miles south of Minehead. The village features in the Domesday Book, which lists it as having forty-one villagers and fifty-two sheep. The Labour politician Ernest Bevin was born here in 1881. In March 2002 Winsford Hill attained notoriety when the still-unidentified body of a man was discovered in black bin bags.

7

Wells, Glastonbury, Wedmore, Chard & Ilminster

Wells Cathedral from the south-east, c. 1906. The first church was built near the wells (which gave the city its name) in 705. In 909 the large diocese of Sherborne was split and the original church became the first Wells Cathedral. The present cathedral building was begun in 1180 on a new site. The best-known feature, the West Front, was completed in about 1260 and features about 300 medieval statues. The famous clock was probably in place by 1390. The reign of Bishop Bekynton (1443–65) saw a great deal of building at the cathedral and, by the time of Henry VIII, the cathedral and all its surrounding buildings were complete as much as they are today.

A view of Wedmore from Mudgley Hill, *c.* 1905. Montague Cooper produced all the Wedmore postcards for Dare and Kerton of Wedmore. The village and parish is almost 5 miles south of Axbridge. It is rumoured that a summer palace of King Alfred stood on Mudgley Hill. The church of St Mary's dominates the village and mostly dates to the fifteenth century, though it may have some earlier parts.

Grants Lane, Wedmore, *c.* 1905. Grants Lane leads on to the Borough which was created in the thirteenth century as a new market area. An electricity generating station was built in Grants Lane in 1908 and was still there as a sub-station until it burnt down in 1999.

The Borough, Wedmore, *c.* 1905. The shop sign here appears to say 'Day Draper'. There were twenty-six entries for the Borough in the 1901 Census and then, like today, it was the centre of Wedmore's commerce. Nowadays the Borough has the added benefit of a shopping mall.

The Borough, Wedmore, *c.* 1905. An interesting aspect of Wedmore's social history is that the Westover family lived there. John Westover was a surgeon and his casebook for 1686 to 1700 still survives. It contains a wealth of local history, families and ailments with contemporary treatments. Westover lists 975 patients; 481 men, 311 women and 183 children. One account states, 'Rebecca Risse of South Brint [*sic*] is pained in her back side and limbs.'

The George Hotel and Church Street, Wedmore, c. 1905. Thomas Hawkins was the hotel proprietor at this time. He was a local man and lived with his wife, Rosina, and two stepchildren. By all accounts the hotel was prosperous as an ostler, domestic servant and a nurse were employed, the latter only twelve years old in 1901. The band seen here is possibly that of the Salvation Army.

John Larder (1817–1909) stands outside his Wedmore cottage, c. 1905. *Kelly's Directory* of 1883 lists John Larder as a stonemason living at Chapel House. In 1896 he and other members of the Methodist Chapel built the Wesleyan Sunday School Room which was opened on 10 April 1896 by the Revd Walford Green. Mr Larder was also a lay minister at the Methodist Chapel and, before her death, his wife Emma was a member for sixty-two years.

Wedmore Flower Show, *c*. 1905. Montague Cooper has captured the heart of the proceedings – the beer tent! An annual flower show is still run at nearby Theale.

The Hall, Sand Road, Wedmore, *c*. 1905. This was home to Alfred Dickinson around this time. In the late 1890s it appears he must have lived in Argentina as two of his children were born there. The household was amply supplied with five servants – a nursery governess, a cook, a nurserymaid, a housemaid and a parlourmaid.

Elmsett Hall, Glanville Street, Wedmore, *c.* 1905. At the time the photograph was taken the hall was owned by Doctor William J. Henson and his wife, Minnie. They had two children and employed a housemaid, a cook and a governess. The hall has now been converted to eleven luxury apartments and a maisonette.

Sexey's School, Blackford, Wedmore, *c.* 1905. Now known as Hugh Sexey Middle School in Sexey's Road. The school takes its name from Hugh Sexey, the son of poor parents living in the Bruton area. In 1599 he was appointed as Royal Auditor to Elizabeth I. The current school was inspired by the Rt Hon. Henry Hobhouse, the first chairman of governors. The school was founded in 1889 as a Trade School, but by the time the photograph was taken had become a boys' grammar school.

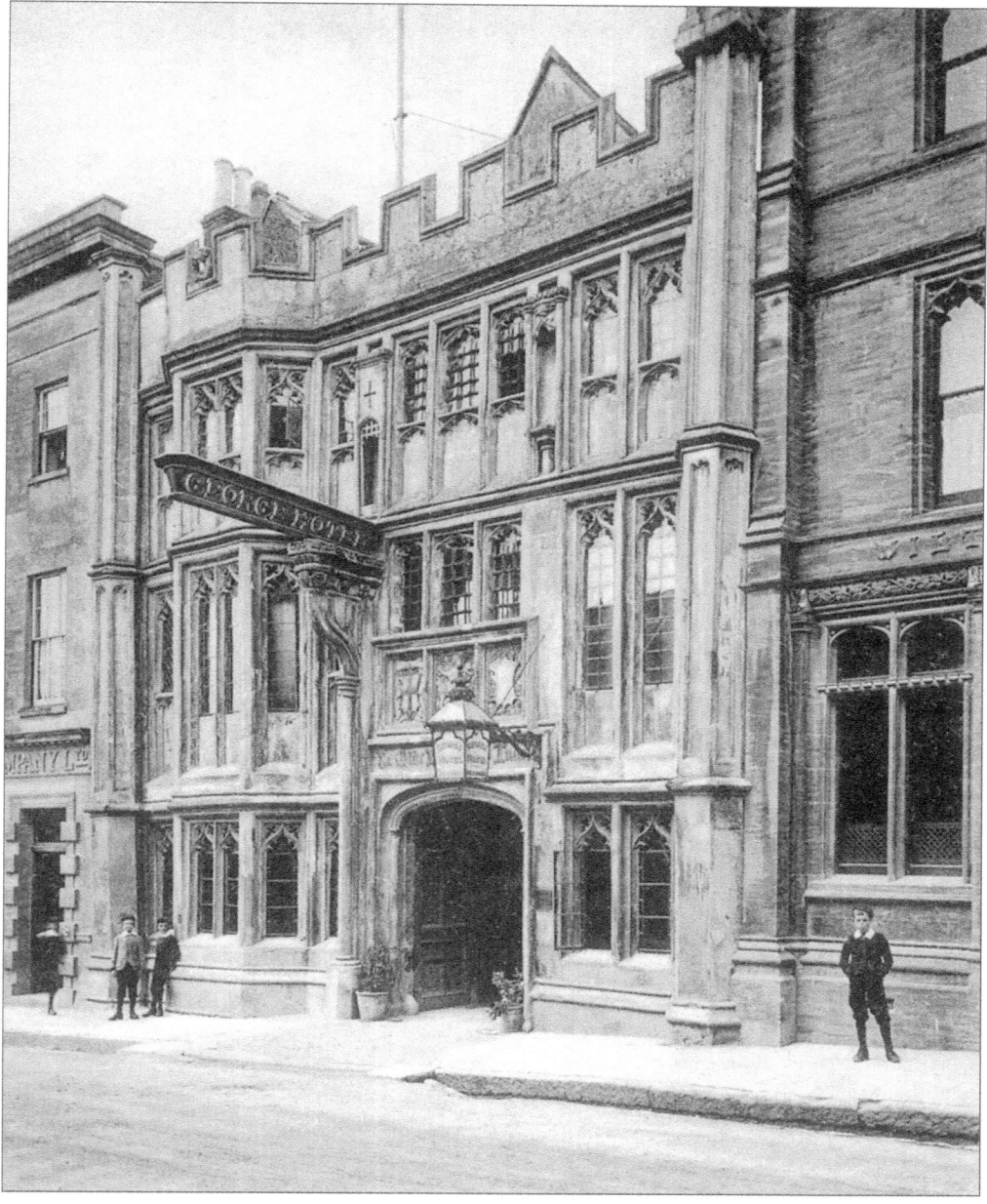

Pilgrims Inn, George Hotel, Glastonbury, *c.* 1906. The inn was built by Abbot Selwood in about 1465 for visitors to Glastonbury. It is one of the finest surviving medieval inns in Britain. In 1901 the inn was managed by Elizabeth Williams and her staff of three 'servants' – a cook, a bookkeeper and a waitress. It seems odd that the 1901 Census categorises employees in establishments such as this as 'servants'.

Glastonbury Abbey. The Abbots Kitchen.

The ruins of Glastonbury Abbey, *c.* 1906. A stone church was established on the site around 712. This church was enlarged in the tenth century by the Abbot of Glastonbury, St Dunstan (later Archbishop of Canterbury). After 1066, the Normans added greatly to the buildings at the abbey and it became the richest in the country. Sadly, all of this was destroyed in a fire in 1184. The medieval monks built a new church and by the fourteenth century the abbey was again one of the richest in the country.

The abbot's kitchen (seen above) is the remaining part of the magnificent abbot's house begun by John de Breynton in the fourteenth century. At the start of the Dissolution of the Monasteries in 1536 there were over 800 monasteries, nunneries and friaries in England. By 1541 there were none.

In 1539 the abbey was stripped of its valuables and the Abbot Richard Whyting was hanged, drawn and quartered as a traitor on Glastonbury Tor.

Wells Market Place, *c.* 1906. Unusually Mr Cooper has given Wrench's postcards a prominent position in this view. The Market Place has been the focal place of the city for centuries. The shops running towards the cathedral are built on walls created by Thomas Bekynton in the fifteenth century. He also provided the water supply here in 1451, which still flows. The Penniless Porch gives access to Cathedral Green.

Harvey's Charity and High Street, Chard, *c.* 1906. Richard Harvey, a merchant of Exeter, in his will, dated 1663, left this property for use as a hospital. It was rebuilt in 1842 and in 2007 a 45-ton crane was used to replace the sixteen chimneys.

United Patriots Procession, Chard, c. 1907. No references have been found for this organisation. This view of High Street shows the spire of the Congregational Church in Fore Street. It was erected in 1868 but became unsafe and was demolished in 1979 to be replaced with shops. Bucklands shop (left) later became Thorne's Drapers and, in later years, the Conservative Club.

Salmet at Chard. French aviator Monsieur Salmet landed at Taunton on 29 May 1912 while taking part in the *Daily Mail* Air Race from South Wales to Chard. Here we see him after his arrival at Chard. Other postcards of the Chard visit were produced by Mr Cooper, including one of the petrol can signed by Salmet, a telegram announcing the aviator's safe arrival in London and the plane flying over a crowd (probably a montage). There was also a close up of Salmet in the cockpit.

South Chard Strict Baptist Chapel stonelaying ceremony, 9 April 1909. The first stone was laid by the pastor, Mr Thomas Dare. A bottle was placed under the stone, containing particulars of the cause and the erection of the new chapel. Also in the bottle was a copy of the articles of faith of the Gospel Standard Society and an issue of *Friendly Companion* for that month.

The completed chapel, 1909. The three deacons all laid a stone each, as did the oldest member of the congregation, Mr J. Bennett. After the ceremony about 130 people sat down for a tea arranged in the old chapel.

A presentation of medals, Chard, 11 April 1909. This took place after the Easter Sunday Church Parade at Cornhill. The Volunteer Long Service Medal was presented by Lieutenant Colonel Gifford to Sergeants Stembridge and Dening, Lance Sergeant Pinney, Corporal Northcott and Private W. Kerle.

Furnham School treat, 1911. Rosie has written this postcard; she is the lady marked 'x' to the left. 'A bit of our procession, we shall see the airships pass here tomorrow.' There were other postcards of this procession. Furnham is the northern part of Chard on the Taunton road.

Wadeford, *c.* 1909. Wadeford is a hamlet in the parish of Combe St Nicholas. The name is supposedly derived from woad, a plant grown for dye. Two streams join here to form the River Isle. There were two mills in the village at this time and the hamlet was quite self-contained with a post office, pub, baker, grocer, blacksmith and shoemaker. In the garden of the large building, the washing is being dried in the old-fashioned way, by laying it on the hedges and bushes.

Chaffcombe coronation festivities, 1911. Village dignitaries assemble here for a coronation photograph. One is surely the Revd Percy Brent MA, recently arrived from Alveley. Chaffcombe is a parish and village 2½ miles north-east of Chard, whose population in 1901 was 228.

An unknown farm in the Chard area, c. 1910. Many of Mr Cooper's cards were uncaptioned. This is such a charming one I have included it in the book. The farmer's dog is seen here taking refuge beneath the cart.

Ash, c. 1906. Ash is a village and parish a mile from Martock, of which it was originally a part. In 1902 the village had a post office and school (for 105 children), a village shop and a hardware dealer. The church is dedicated to the Holy Trinity. The population in 1891 was 461 people, mostly engaged in agriculture.

A general view of Ilminster, *c.* 1906. The town is an urban district and the population in 1901 was 3,135. At this time the town had a small brewery, large flax and tow works, a lace manufactory, rope, brick and tile works together with shirt and collar factories. The brewery was in West Street trading as J. Paull from 1859 to about 1890 when it became J. Paull & Son.

Dillington House, *c.* 1906. The main house dates back to the sixteenth century and it is considered to be one of the most beautiful in Somerset. At this time the park amounted to nearly 47 acres. It was the seat of Lieutenant Colonel Arthur Vaughan Hanning Vaughan-Lee JP, Lord of the Manor and chief landowner in the area. Dillington House is now run by Somerset County Council as a residential centre for professional development.

Ilminster Girls' Grammar School, *c.* 1906. The sender of this card has written, 'This is where I go to the County Cooking Courses 9 til 12.30 Saturdays. We have ranges, gas stoves and all the latest utensils.' The Girls' Grammar School was established in 1879 in the Old School House, built in 1586. It had rooms for teaching practical cookery and modern additions for school purposes.

Court Barton, Ilminster. This is still a quiet part of Ilminster where the Abbots of Muchelney held sway for some five centuries. The Old Grammar School buildings are here together with Crosse House and the Chantry with its fifteenth-century doorway. St Mary's Church, or the Minster as it is known, remains one of the finest parish churches in the country.

Marshalsea Brothers, Ilminster, *c*. 1910. Ernest A. Marshalsea, a coach painter, had a coachbuilding business in East Street, Ilminster, in about 1905. Together with his brother, he formed a coach and motor works in Ilminster in about 1908. Around 1910, Marshalseas were appointed sole local agents for the Bristol-based company Straker-Squire. It seems likely that they added their own bodies to the 15hp Mark One or Mark Two models. E.A. Marshalsea lived at Whitelackington in 1902 with his wife, daughter and a young servant. The brothers opened a garage in Taunton before January 1911 (*see* page 11).

Buckland House, Buckland St Mary, *c*. 1909. The old gardener works in the background while in the foreground are the family children and their pets. In 1910 this was the residence of the Revd Alfred Percival Pott MA.

The Girls' Friendly Society at an unknown Somerset location, c. 1909. The society was founded in England by Mary Elizabeth Townsend in 1875. Its purpose was to support women in the Church of England who were not married and who had been sent by their families to the city to work in textile mills. It was also to experience friendship and recreation in a fellowship of Christian love and service. Today, the society is a national volunteer organisation in the Episcopal Church for young girls from the ages of five to twenty-one.

48th Siege Battery Royal Garrison Artillery (RGA), 1915. In 1899 the Royal Artillery was divided into two distinct branches: mounted and dismounted. The RGA was established as a separate corps from Royal Horse Artillery and Royal Field Artillery. The heavy and siege batteries manned the big guns – notably 9.2in howitzers. Only Alfred Benjamin Street is identified in the photograph. He was born in India in about 1887.

The Gloucestershire Royal Field Artillery at Berrow, *c.* 1915. Shown here are the lighter guns of the Royal Field Artillery. Field guns fired their shells on a flat trajectory and were of use over open ground, while the howitzers and mortars fired in an arc and were of use when the enemy was obscured. These are QF (quick-firing) 15lb guns, of an older design dating back to the 1890s. They were poor battlefield weapons but proved useful in a training role. They could fire a 14lb shell 3¼ miles. Mr Cooper produced a number of cards featuring these exercises.

A mystery photograph, *c.* 1912. This one has totally eluded the author. It looks to be a congregation outside a chapel building. Hopefully a reader will identify the location.

Acknowledgements

This collection of photographs by Henry Montague Cooper has been formed by myself over a thirty-year period. I would like to thank the great many postcard dealers who have helped me in my quest. Family history has been supplied by Mr Cooper's grandson, Anthony Paines. He also supplied the photographs of Mr Cooper and his daughters. Caption information has kindly been supplied by Neville Upham, Kathleen Hill, Mike White and the staff at the Somerset Local Studies Library. The author was very lucky to talk to the late Mrs Paradine, née Phillips, who worked for Mr Cooper at Taunton and bought all his glass negatives (since destroyed). If others can add information or examples of Mr Cooper's work, the author would be happy to hear from them via the publisher.

An early Montague Cooper cabinet card, *c.* 1886. The business is referred to as H.M. Cooper, late Morley. Later Mr Cooper adopted the name of Montague Cooper for business purposes.